Tax Delinquency in the Inner City

Tax Delinquency in the Inner City

The Problem and Its Possible Solutions

Susan Olson
Cleveland City Planning
Commission

M. Leanne Lachman
Real Estate Research
Corporation

Lexington Books
D.C. Heath and Company
Lexington, Massachusetts
Toronto

Library of Congress Cataloging in Publication Data

Olson, Susan.
    Tax delinquency in the inner city.

    1. Property tax—Cleveland. 2. Tax collection—Cleveland. 3.
Foreclosure—Cleveland. I. Lachman, M. Leanne, joint author. II.
Title.
HJ9298.C62038   336.2'009767'69   76-20399
ISBN 0-669-00887-7

The preparation of this document was financed in part through Comprehensive Planning Grant CPA-OH-05-16-0337 from the U.S. Department of Housing and Urban Development, under the provision of Section 701 of the Housing Act of 1954, as amended. Cleveland City Planning Commission, 501 City Hall, Cleveland, Ohio 44114

Published simultaneously in Canada

Printed in the United States of America

International Standard Book Number: 0-669-00887-7

Library of Congress Catalog Card Number: 76-20399

For Norman Krumholz

Contents

List of Figures — ix

List of Tables — xi

Acknowledgments — xv

Introduction — 1

Chapter 1 ⸀ **Tax Delinquency: The Nature of the Problem** — 7

The Changing Nature of Cleveland's Tax Delinquency — 7
Overview of Cleveland — 9
The Extent of Cleveland's Tax Delinquency — 17
Geographic Areas of Concentrated Delinquency — 20
Value of Tax Delinquent Parcels — 27

Chapter 2 ⸀ **Cleveland's Property Tax–Foreclosure Process** — 33

The Steps in Foreclosure — 34
Results of Recent Tax Sales — 40
Sale Revenues in Relation to Costs — 44
Tax Status of Foreclosed Delinquent Parcels After Sale — 47
Conclusions — 49

Chapter 3 **A Model for Change: St. Louis's Land Reutilization Authority** — 53

Structure of the St. Louis LRA — 55
The St. Louis Tax-Foreclosure Process — 57
The LRA's Property Management Capabilities — 59
The LRA's Operating Experience — 60
The Jackson County/Kansas City Foreclosure Process — 62
Conclusions — 64

Chapter 4 **Classification of Cleveland's Residential Neighborhoods** — 67

Five-Stage Classification of Residential Areas — 68
Population and Housing Characteristics — 76

	Tax Delinquency Trends in Residential Areas	79
	Neighborhoods Selected for the Survey	82
Chapter 5	**Characteristics of Cleveland's Tax Delinquent Parcels**	85
	Survey Methodology	85
	Delinquent Property Survey Findings	87
	Survey Implications	106
Chapter 6	**The Fragile Inner-City Housing Market**	109
	The U. S. Urban Development Process	110
	Survey of Large-Scale Landlords	113
	Cleveland's Tax Delinquent Property-Owners	122
Chapter 7	**Conclusions and Recommendations**	129
	Issue 1: How Can Administrative Costs of Tax Foreclosure Be Decreased, and Efficiency Increased, While Still Protecting the Rights of Property-Owners?	132
	Issue 2: How Can the City and Other Taxing Districts be Compensated for Lost Tax Revenues and Property Maintenance Expenditures?	134
	Issue 3: Should a Municipal Land Reutilization Program Acquire Occupied Residential Properties?	137
	Issue 4: How Can Any Hardships Imposed on Residential Property-Owners as a Result of Foreclosure Be Minimized?	138
Appendix A	**Miscellaneous Supplementary Tables**	142
Appendix B	**Summary of Ohio H.B. 1327 as Enacted Into Law**	151
	About the Authors	159

List of Figures

1–1   Change in Assessed Valuation of Real Property—City of Cleveland, Suburban County Area, and Cuyahoga County, 1960 and 1974   17

1–2   Delinquent Parcels as a Percent of Total Properties in Cleveland Statistical Areas, 1966–1974   24

2–1   Administrative Procedure for Foreclosing on Tax Delinquent Properties in Cuyahoga County   36

4–1   The Neighborhood Change Continuum   71

4–2   Stages of Neighborhood Development of City of Cleveland's Residential Areas   74

4–3   Tax Delinquent Parcels, West Hough, 1974   81

5–1   Inventory of Vacant and Cleared Properties, West Hough, 1975   91

List of Tables

1–1   City of Cleveland and SMSA Population, 1950–1970   11

1–2   Racial Composition of Cleveland's Population, 1950– 1970   11

1–3   Number of Major Crimes Committed in the City of Cleveland and Rates per 100,000 Residents, 1965–1974   12

1–4   Number of Major Crimes Committed in Cleveland's East and West Sides in 1974   13

1–5   Local Taxes and Total General Fund Operating Revenues for the City of Cleveland, 1969–1974   18

1–6   Real and Public Utility Tax Delinquency in the City of Cleveland, 1966–1974   18

1–7   Geographic Distribution of Delinquent Property Tax Dollars in the City of Cleveland in 1974   21

1–8   Location of Delinquent Parcels in the City of Cleveland, 1966 and 1974   22

1–9   Number of Delinquent Parcels in the City of Cleveland, 1966–1974   22

1–10   Delinquency Rates in Central East Side Statistical Areas of Cleveland, 1966–1974   23

1–11   Delinquency Rates in Peripheral Statistical Areas of Cleveland's East Side, 1966–1974   27

1–12   Delinquency Rates in Selected West Side Statistical Areas, 1966–1974   28

1–13   Assessed Valuation of Delinquent Property in Cleveland in 1974   29

2–1   Length of Delinquency of City of Cleveland Parcels, as of 1974   38

2–2   Disposition of Cleveland Parcels at Sheriff's Sales of Tax-Foreclosed Properties, 1969–1974   40

2–3   Disposition of Cleveland Parcels at Auditor's Sales of Forfeited Properties, 1969 and 1972   41

2–4   Prices Obtained for Tax Delinquent Cleveland Properties at Sheriff's Sales, 1969–1974   42

2–5   Sales-to-Market-Value Ratios for Cleveland Properties Sold at Sheriff's Sales, 1969–1974   42

2–6	Prices Paid for Cleveland Parcels at 1969 and 1972 Forfeiture Sales	43
2–7	Sales-to-Market-Value Ratios for Cleveland Properties Sold at 1969 and 1972 Forfeiture Sales	43
2–8	Quantifiable Administrative Costs for Cleveland Parcels Sold at Sheriff's Sales, 1969–1974	45
2–9	Recovery of Delinquent Taxes and Administrative Costs on Cleveland Parcels Offered at Sheriff's Sales, 1969–1971	46
2–10	Forfeiture Sale Prices as a Percent of Delinquent Taxes Due, 1969 and 1972	47
4–1	Characteristics of Neighborhoods in the Five General Stages on the Change Continuum	72
4–2	Selected Population, Housing, and Tax Delinquency Data for the City of Cleveland's Residential Statistical Areas	75
5–1	Characteristics of Delinquent Parcels in the City of Cleveland, by Stage of Neighborhood Development	88
5–2	Percent of Delinquent Parcels in the City of Cleveland and Selected Statistical Areas That Are Vacant	89
5–3	Tax Delinquent Parcels on the City of Cleveland's 1974 Demolition List	92
5–4	Condition of Unoccupied Structures on Surveyed Tax Delinquent Properties, by Stage of Neighborhood Development	92
5–5	Surveyed Delinquent Parcels Containing Unoccupied Structures, by Use of Structure	93
5–6	Percent of Delinquent Parcels That Contain Occupied Residential Structures, by Stage of Neighborhood Development	95
5–7	Size Distribution of Occupied Residential Structures Surveyed, by Stage of Neighborhood Development	96
5–8	Number of Units in Delinquent Occupied Residential Structures Surveyed, by Stage of Neighborhood Development	97
5–9	Distribution of Delinquent, Owner- and Renter-Occupied Structures, by Stage of Neighborhood Development	99

5–10	Percent of Delinquent Occupied Residential Structures That Were Renter-Occupied in 1975	100
5–11	Percent of All Housing Units That Were Renter-Occupied in 1970	100
5–12	Relative and Absolute Physical Condition of Total Occupied Delinquent Structures	101
5–13	Relative and Absolute Physical Condition of Owner-Occupied Delinquent Structures	104
5–14	Relative and Absolute Physical Condition of Total Vacant Delinquent Structures	105
6–1	1975 Pro Forma Operating Statements for Older Low- and Middle-Income Apartment Buildings in Cleveland	117
6–2	Relative Importance of Operating Problems of Inner-City Landlords in Cleveland and Newark	119
6–3	Estimated Distribution of Cleveland's Delinquent Housing Units Among Key Types of Property-Owners	123
6–4	Approximate Ownership Pattern of Lower-Income Delinquent Housing Units in Cleveland in 1975	125
A–1	Population and Housing Characteristics, by Neighborhood Type, for Cleveland's Residential Statistical Areas	142
A–2	Total Number of Tax Delinquent Parcels, by Residential Statistical Area	144
A–3	Families Receiving Aid to Dependent Children (ADC) in Cleveland's Residential Statistical Areas	146
A–4	Vacant Delinquent Land in Field Survey Neighborhoods	148
A–5	Relative and Absolute Physical Condition of Occupied Delinquent Residential Structures	149
A–6	Relative and Absolute Physical Condition of Vacant Delinquent Residential Structures	149
A–7	Surveyed Tax Delinquent Parcels With Occupied Structures, by Use of Structure	150

Acknowledgments

We appreciate the support that The Cleveland Foundation gave to this research project. The foundation provided the funds for consultant participation in the study, and the City Planning Commission staff work was funded in large part through a Section 701 Comprehensive Planning Grant from the U.S. Department of Housing and Urban Development.

A number of people on the Cleveland City Planning Commission staff contributed to this study. Norman Krumholz, Executive Director, provided advice and encouragement in his capacity as project codirector. Craig Miller and Ronald Isaac made the initial inquiries into the legal aspects of Ohio's foreclosure procedures. John Linner assisted in designing research techniques, analyzing data, and developing final conclusions. Stephen Szanto, Roy Williams, William Goodson, Walter Howard, Kevin Reichley, Larry Vana, Steve Cohan, Harley Cahen, and Ruth Ann O'Leary gathered much of the information used in this study. Keki Dadachanji, Warsella Thompson, and Helen Gottschalk performed the data processing, and Amanda Andahazy assisted with the preparation of the graphics. Nadine Lane, Sandra Wilson, and Eugene Piunno provided secretarial assistance.

Three Real Estate Research Corporation staff members carried out special research projects that contributed significantly to the content and conclusions of this study. Maxine V. Mitchell performed the classification of Cleveland neighborhoods and participated in the analysis of all the data collected for the study. J. Terrence Farris analyzed the St. Louis Land Reutilization Authority and the Jackson County Land Trust, and J. Denis Gathman performed the interviews with large-scale inner-city landlords in Cleveland.

John C. Dowd and R. Thomas Stanton of Squire, Sanders & Dempsey served as legal consultants and drafted the legislation described in Chapter 7.

Mayor Ralph J. Perk and City Council President George Forbes encouraged the City Planning Commission to undertake this study and provided support throughout its course.

We would also like to extend our appreciation to George Voinovich, Auditor of Cuyahoga County. Without his cooperation and the assistance of Vincent Lombardi, Edwin Sawicki, and other members of his staff, the task of completing this study would have been much more difficult.

The Planning Commission staff wishes to thank the members of the Cleveland City Planning Commission: Wallace Teare, Chairman; James B. Davis; Allen Fonoroff; Herman P. Goldsmith; Councilman Gerald T. McFaul; Reverend Daniel F. Reidy; and R. Joyce Whitley. Without their support, this research could never have been undertaken.

Introduction

X Property tax delinquency is reaching serious proportions in urban areas throughout the United States. It is only one of the symptoms—and effects—of the bundle of problems that became known in the mid-1960s as the "urban crisis." Unlike most of its complementary problems, however, tax delinquency has a direct, readily perceivable financial impact. School boards, county governments, and cities rely in varying degrees upon property tax revenues, and the erosion of any revenue source heightens their financial squeeze.

Tax delinquency can also have significant indirect effects. To compensate for lost revenues from delinquent parcels, property tax rates are usually raised—unless they are already at the legal limits, in which case another type of tax is increased. Therefore owners of nondelinquent properties are generally required to pay higher taxes to maintain the level of revenues. Some property-owners may find this difficult, and delinquency may increase further. Also, since property taxes are one of the many factors considered by homeowners and investors when evaluating possible locations, increased central-city taxes create a disincentive for new or continued ownership of real estate within the municipal boundaries. When this is manifest by lack of demand for property, values stabilize and eventually decline, reducing the city's tax base. This in turn creates more fiscal problems, which can lead to further property tax increases and a reiteration of the same disinvestment cycle.

There were over 11,000 tax delinquent parcels in the city of Cleveland in 1974, up from 8200 in 1966. Delinquent taxes and public liens on these properties totaled $23 million. The delinquency rate for the city as a whole was 6.5 percent in 1974, but almost one-third of the total parcels in the inner-city area of West Hough were delinquent at that time. Other older northeastern cities have comparable quantities of delinquency, especially in their more deteriorated areas; and central cities in the Midwest, South, and West are also experiencing increases in property tax delinquency.

The recent rapid growth of tax delinquency in Cleveland has been centered in deteriorating inner-city residential neighborhoods. The weak—and in some cases collapsing—real estate markets in these areas have rendered the existing foreclosure process ineffective. Foreclosed properties usually cannot be sold at prices sufficient to cover the back taxes, and the proceeds often do not cover even the administrative costs of the sale. The purchasers of these foreclosed properties, many of whom are land speculators, frequently do not pay taxes either, so the properties simply reappear on delinquency lists. Thus continued use of the current

1

foreclosure procedure, with its high administrative costs, serves only to increase governments' unrecoverable investments in delinquent parcels.

The study described in this book was undertaken in Cleveland to develop recommendations for changes in state legislation that would enable metropolitan counties with declining inner-city areas to handle foreclosure more effectively. To arrive at such recommendations, it was necessary to learn a great deal about the nature of tax delinquency and the properties usually associated with it.

Causes of Contemporary Tax Delinquency

Tax delinquency is accelerating in declining inner-city areas. Social problems and an older building stock have made central cities unattractive to many residents and businesses, and high volumes of new suburban construction have created appealing locational alternatives. The outmigration of middle- and upper-income households from central cities to the suburbs has loosened inner-city housing markets, and vacancy rates have become high in the most deteriorated residential neighborhoods. Operating costs of apartment buildings have risen much faster than rent-paying capabilities of low-income tenants. Thus many rental buildings are no longer profitable investments. Property values have therefore declined, and large numbers of buildings and vacant lots in some cities now have *no* value. There has been a sharp increase in the volume of abandoned buildings, many of which are tax delinquent.

Owners often stop paying taxes long before their properties are abandoned. Landlords may find nonpayment of taxes a convenient way to reduce their expenses, and homeowners may be forced to use their limited funds for more pressing needs. Tax delinquent owners are frequently aware that the foreclosure process is a long one. Some hope to accumulate the money to redeem their properties at a future time; others view nonpayment of taxes as a means of improving the cash flow of properties they do not plan to redeem. In cities where the foreclosure process moves slowly—whether for legal or administrative reasons, or both—owners soon learn that they will not be in danger of losing their properties for many years. This knowledge presumably increases the incidence of tax delinquency.

Another type of tax delinquency arises when investors purposely postpone payment of holding costs until they sell their vacant land. In these cases the taxes and the penalty for delinquency are paid at the time of sale. Similar situations arise when investors postpone property tax payments because they have temporary cash flow difficulties. This type of deferral becomes more common when interest rates on short-term loans exceed the penalty rates for tax delinquency. Real estate investors who deliberately delay tax payments are irritating to tax collectors, but they are not part of a long-term tax delinquency problem.

Effects of Prolonged Tax Delinquency

In taxing jurisdictions where the percentage of delinquent properties is increasing significantly, the primary cause is usually weakening real estate markets. Such rises in delinquency have a number of attendant adverse effects. Key among these are the following:

1. In most jurisdictions, nondelinquent taxpayers are forced to assume the financial burden created by property owners who are not paying their taxes. This is true if property tax rates are raised to maintain revenues, or if services to all property-owners are reduced in accord with lower tax receipts.
2. Administrative costs for tax collection increase substantially. Normal costs rise per tax dollar generated because the same billing procedure brings in less revenue. Additional costs are also incurred when the foreclosure process is initiated and carried out on a larger volume of properties. Furthermore, in a declining real estate market, the eventual foreclosure sales are unlikely to recover either the administrative costs or the accumulated delinquent taxes.
3. The fiscal problems of the taxing bodies increase because of reduced revenues, added costs, and tax base erosion.
4. To a considerable degree, tax delinquency is a precursor to property abandonment. Though not all abandoned properties are tax delinquent prior to abandonment, high rates of delinquency have been found to correlate with eventual abandonment.
5. Tax delinquency in weak real estate markets creates property disposition and management problems for local governments. Often there are no purchasers at tax sales. Local government expenditures for public health and safety activities also increase for demolition of condemned buildings, repair of broken utility lines, trash removal from vacant lots, and police and fire protection necessitated by crime and vandalism in vacant buildings. In addition, local governments can end up owning a great deal of vacant land. There is also the potential, as discussed in Chapter 6, for public acquisition of occupied buildings that have been abandoned by their owners. The possible costs and political implications of such ownership or management are frightening.

The magnitude of each of the above effects will vary with the relative size and affluence of taxing districts and municipalities. Increasing tax delinquency can signal the beginning of a growing trend of casual or deferred payment that will be stopped only with radical action. More often, however, it is merely a symptom of a collapsing real estate market. Legal and administrative actions can then reduce or control only some of these effects. Carefully considered revisions of the foreclosure process, however, could improve the system's efficiency and provide some compensation for lost tax revenues.

Design of the Cleveland Study

In response to the negative effects of Cleveland's growing tax delinquency, the City Planning Commission began an analysis of the nature and extent of property tax delinquency in the city and a review of the foreclosure process followed in Cuyahoga County (the tax-administering jurisdiction). After preliminary reconnaissance work was completed, the Planning Commission obtained a grant from the Cleveland Foundation to perform a more detailed examination of the problem and to develop recommendations for legal and administrative changes in the foreclosure process. A study team was assembled, consisting of City Planning Commission staff members, Real Estate Research Corporation, and the law firm of Squire, Sanders & Dempsey.

The intent of the Cleveland study was to propose changes in Ohio state tax foreclosure laws directed toward (1) strengthening the disincentives against tax delinquency and abandonment; (2) providing some compensations to local governments for lost tax revenues and maintenance expenditures; (3) streamlining the foreclosure process to minimize administrative costs while still protecting the rights of property owners; and (4) creating a mechanism to assist local governments in eventually redeveloping cleared, tax delinquent land.

Originally the staff anticipated that the study would lead to recommended creation in Ohio of an optional rapid foreclosure process similar to that instituted in Missouri in 1971. The Missouri law enabled St. Louis to accelerate foreclosure and created a Land Reutilization Authority, which takes title to delinquent properties that fail to sell for at least the amount of the delinquent taxes. As described in Chapter 3, this system has become a model that is being considered by many states and taxing jurisdictions who face heightened tax delinquency and weakening inner-city real estate markets.

When we surveyed tax delinquent parcels in the city of Cleveland, we found that many parcels were vacant and could be transferred to public ownership to be held for future redevelopment without increasing the city's management responsibilities significantly. We also found, however, that a high proportion of the delinquent properties were occupied residential buildings in low-income areas, many of which were owner-occupied. Public acquisition of these parcels would present both political and fiscal problems because the city would become the landlord of last resort for many low-income residents living in deteriorating structures.

The findings from the tax delinquency survey in Cleveland led us to conclude that two separate approaches should be followed in foreclosing on inner-city properties. A rapid process should be instituted for vacant parcels wherein the city would take title to the parcels that could not be sold for at least the amount of delinquent taxes. The city would then "bank" the parcels until they could be aggregated for disposition, when reuse potential developed. This process would significantly reduce the administrative costs of foreclosure for vacant parcels and would provide the public with some form of compensation for lost tax revenues and maintenance expenditures. We also concluded, however, that it would not be desirable for the city to receive occupied residential buildings. The foreclosure process for these properties would remain essentially the same as it is now. To reduce the costs connected with that process, we recommended a number of statutory changes in the administrative requirements. We also suggested that the county treasurer undertake stronger informal collection efforts to increase tax payment by delinquent owners who had suffered only temporary financial difficulties. The specific conclusions and recommendations that resulted from the Cleveland study are presented in Chapter 7.

Because there has been relatively little close analysis of the growing tax delinquency problem in America's central cities, we believe that this study offers basic information and methodological suggestions that will be useful in other cities. We have also developed an alternative model for change that is a modification of the Missouri, or St. Louis, plan. Depending on the interests of particular readers, some chapters of this book may be of greater importance than others. The issues covered in Chapters 2 through 7 are summarized at the end of Chapter 1.

Tax Delinquency: The Nature of the Problem

Tax delinquency has become an increasingly serious problem in the city of Cleveland in the last ten years, as it has in a number of other older central cities. Property in deteriorated areas of the city is becoming delinquent at alarming rates as owner disinvestment and abandonment accelerate. City expenditures for maintenance of abandoned property, such as those for demolition of condemned structures, have also been increasing. These appear on the tax duplicate as liens against the properties when owners fail to reimburse the city. Dramatic changes in the distribution of population and wealth within the metropolitan area have negatively influenced both the magnitude of Cleveland's tax base and the rate of tax collection.

Over 11,000 parcels in Cleveland, or 6.5 percent of the city's total properties, were delinquent by 1974. This represents a rise in delinquency of almost 37 percent since 1966. The increase in the dollar value of outstanding delinquent taxes was much greater—growing from $5.4 million in 1966 to almost $23 million by 1974. Approximately $10 million of the 1974 taxes was owed by the Penn Central Transportation Company.[a] Tax delinquency is only one of the fiscal problems confronting Cleveland's administrators, but its rapid growth in recent years has made a clear understanding of its characteristics much more crucial.

This chapter focuses on the extent of tax delinquency and the changing nature of delinquent parcels in Cuyahoga County and the city of Cleveland. It provides the background for the detailed analysis and search for remedial solutions that are described in later chapters. It also includes a brief description of the economic condition of the city of Cleveland because the overall health of the city is both a cause and an effect of tax delinquency.

The Changing Nature of Cleveland's Tax Delinquency

Historically, real property tax delinquency occurred primarily in the suburbs of Cuyahoga County. The city of Cleveland was surrounded on three sides by vast amounts of undeveloped land, much of which was not

---

[a]Because of the bankruptcy of the Penn Central Transportation Company, the delinquent taxes on properties in Cleveland and other cities are not collectible.

served by public water or sewers and therefore had limited marketability. Owners of large tracts of land, who were often unable to sell or improve their properties, allowed them to become tax delinquent. As a result, the suburbs of Cuyahoga County experienced a more severe property tax delinquency problem than did the city of Cleveland.

The Regional Association of Cleveland undertook an in-depth study of real property tax delinquency in Cuyahoga County in 1940, when the county was facing serious delinquency in the aftermath of the Depression. In the 1933 tax collection, almost 60 percent of the real property in the county was delinquent. Although the situation had improved by 1940, over 40 percent of the parcels in the county remained delinquent. At the same time, however, only 29 percent of the parcels in the city of Cleveland were delinquent. Delinquency rates in other older, developed suburban communities were also lower than those in the primarily undeveloped fringe areas of the county. Almost one-half of the county's real estate parcels were located in the city of Cleveland, but only one-third of the delinquent parcels and about 28 percent of the dollar value of delinquent taxes were attributable to the city.[1] In both the city and county, the overwhelming majority of the delinquent land was vacant. In Cleveland, 91.5 percent of the chronically delinquent parcels—the parcels that had been delinquent for four years or more—were vacant. Despite the large number of delinquent parcels, only a small portion of the total assessed valuation was delinquent because many of the delinquent parcels were unimproved and therefore had low values.[b]

The pattern of real property tax delinquency in Cuyahoga County has changed radically in recent years. The problem that was once more serious in the suburbs has now disproportionately afflicted the central city. Much of the land in the suburbs has been developed since 1940, and property tax delinquency has declined significantly. At the same time, a number of the city's neighborhoods have experienced heavy deterioration and, in some cases, extensive abandonment. Property tax delinquency is rising rapidly in these areas, and the problem is spreading to neighborhoods in initial stages of decline.

In 1975, over two-thirds of the $32.6 million in delinquent real and public utility property taxes in the county were due on property located in the city of Cleveland. The property tax levy in the city of Cleveland supports the county, the city, and the Cleveland Board of Education, so three governmental bodies have an interest in the collection of delinquent taxes. In the 1974 tax year, the real property tax rate in the city was 69 mills: 42.2 mills levied by the board of education, 11.7 mills by Cuyahoga

---

[b]A property's assessed valuation is the value that is used to compute the property taxes. In the 1970s in Cuyahoga County, assessed valuation has been approximately one-third of market value.

County, and 15.1 mills by the city of Cleveland. The Cleveland Board of Education would stand to gain the most if all delinquent taxes due on property located in the city were to be recovered. As of the 1973 tax year, the board of education would have been entitled to $12.4 million if the total delinquent taxes on city properties had been collected; the city of Cleveland would have received $4.5 million; and Cuyahoga County would have gained $3 million.

The county auditor has estimated that only 19 percent of the delinquent taxes will ever be paid.[2] As properties remain delinquent for long periods and taxes accumulate, the value of the land and buildings often decreases because of weakening market conditions. The possibility of tax collection therefore becomes more and more remote as overdue taxes come to represent an increasingly higher percentage of market value.

Overview of Cleveland

Rising tax delinquency is only one of a complex of interrelated problems facing the city of Cleveland, so a look at some of the other important forces at work is necessary to understand the delinquency phenomenon. Cleveland's problems are similar to those of many other older central cities. Unemployment, poverty, racial transition, and crime are increasing. The city's physical plant is deteriorating, and replacement investments are being made for the most part in the suburbs rather than the city. The ongoing exodus of both jobs and residents from the central city has resulted in rapid suburban growth and concomitant emergence of urban wastelands within the city itself. As a consequence, the city's declining tax base has not been adequate to generate the money needed to maintain full municipal services. This scenario is familiar to students of urban problems. Central cities across the nation are in a similar financial squeeze, and many of them are steadily declining.

The Cleveland metropolitan area, which includes Cuyahoga, Geauga, Lake, and Medina Counties, has over two million residents, about one-third of whom live in the 76-square-mile central city. Cleveland is an industrial city located in the middle of the Great Lakes manufacturing belt—on the south shore of Lake Erie approximately 350 miles east of Chicago and 500 miles west of New York City. Because of its excellent access to both raw materials and markets, Cleveland's economy leans heavily toward production of durable goods, particularly steel. Although steel manufacturing is the most prominent industry in the area, the industrial base is diversified. Other important manufactured products include machine tools, fabricated metals, automotive parts, electric motors, petroleum products, and chemicals.

Cleveland's specialization in heavy industry has been of great histori-
cal advantage. Manufacturing firms have traditionally paid relatively high
wages for unskilled and semiskilled labor, and the concentration of industrial activity in Cleveland meant that many workers without special skills
could earn an adequate income. Manufacturing is, however, no longer a
rapidly growing sector of the national economy. Furthermore, the indus-
tries most important to Cleveland are growing less rapidly than the manufacturing sector as a whole. Although employment in manufacturing rose
by 21.3 percent nationally from 1958 to 1970 (as compared to 38.6 percent
for trade, 70.6 percent for services, and 59.9 percent for government), the
increase in the Cleveland metropolitan area was only 10.8 percent.

Within the Cleveland region, the locus of economic activity is shifting
from the central city to the suburbs. During the 1960s, the number of jobs
located in the city dropped by 71,000, a loss of 15.4 percent. The remainder of Cuyahoga County added 110,000 jobs between 1960 and 1970—a
gain of 73.2 percent.

Population Trends

Cleveland's total population is falling rapidly. As shown in Table 1-1, it
dropped by 38,750 persons in the 1950s and then by 125,150 persons in the
1960s. The rate of decline in the 1970s appears to be close to that of the
1960 to 1970 period. The Cleveland City Planning Commission estimated
that the city population was approximately 690,000 persons in 1975, as
compared to 751,000 in 1970. In large part, the population decline reflects
suburbanization because the portion of the metropolitan area beyond the
central city has grown steadily since 1950. While Cleveland was losing
164,000 residents between 1950 and 1970, the remainder of the Standard
Metropolitan Statistical Area (SMSA) was gaining nearly 700,000 persons.

Cleveland's racial composition has also changed dramatically since
1950. In that year, blacks represented 16.2 percent of the city's population; the figure had risen to 38.3 percent by 1970. Over the same period, as
shown in Table 1-2, the total black population nearly doubled while the
nonblack population dropped by about 40 percent. Although Cleveland's
black population grew during the 1960s, the increase was attributable to
an excess of births over deaths rather than to inmigration. According to
calculations by the City Planning Commission, Cleveland experienced net
outmigration of both blacks and whites.

The Cuyahoga River divides Cleveland into two parts—the East Side
and the West Side—and most city residents consider themselves either
East Siders or West Siders. In 1970, 98 percent of the West Side's 280,904

Table 1–1
City of Cleveland and SMSA Population, 1950–1970

	1950	1960	1970
City of Cleveland	914,808	876,050	750,903
Remainder of Cleveland SMSA	617,766	1,033,434	1,313,291
Total Cleveland SMSA	1,532,574	1,909,484	2,064,194

Source: U.S. Bureau of the Census.

residents were white, whereas 61 percent of the East Side's 469,963 residents were black. Thus nearly all the black residents are concentrated in one area; the Cuyahoga River divides the City of Cleveland racially as well as geographically.

As in nearly all other major central cities, Cleveland's residents, on average, are less affluent than the residents of surrounding suburbs. In 1970, the median family income was $9107 in Cleveland and $12,704 in the rest of the metropolitan area. One of every two Cleveland families ranked in the bottom one-third of the income distribution for all families in the SMSA. Moreover, a large and growing proportion of the city's population depends on public assistance. One out of every five Cleveland families received Aid to Dependent Children (ADC) in 1975.[3] The population losses from outmigration have been heaviest among the more affluent segments of the population. In 1960 there were 81,000 families in the city with incomes above the SMSA's median. This number had fallen to 62,000 by 1970. In ten years, therefore, Cleveland lost 23 percent of its families with above-average incomes.

The implications of these trends are clear: Cleveland is losing its middle class, and the remaining population is less and less able to pay the costs of public or private goods and services.

Table 1–2
Racial Composition of Cleveland's Population, 1950–1970

	1950		1960		1970	
	Number	%	Number	%	Number	%
Blacks	147,847	16.2%	250,818	28.6%	287,841	38.3%
Whites and others	766,961	83.8	625,232	71.4	463,062	61.7
Total population	914,808	100.0%	876,050	100.0%	750,903	100.0%

Source: U.S. Bureau of the Census.

Crime

A major factor in the reduction of jobs and residents in Cleveland is unquestionably the rapidly rising crime rates and the citizens' accompanying—and perhaps exaggerated—perception of danger. As part of the city's Community Renewal Program, a survey of over 3700 Cleveland households was conducted in 1970 in which interviewees were asked to name the three biggest problems facing the city. Over 73 percent cited crime and violence in the streets as one of the three most serious problems. No other single item or issue was mentioned by even half the respondents.[4] The figures in Table 1–3 testify to the marked increase in crime in the city between 1965 and 1974. The rate of reported crimes per 100,000 persons at least doubled in nine years for every category of major crime except larceny. It is safe to assume that the incidence was actually higher since many people do not report crimes such as rape, assault, larceny, and breaking and entering. Cleveland's crime rates are not particularly exceptional among large central cities, though the rates for violent crimes are higher than those for property crimes and place Cleveland in the top half dozen or so large cities where crime is most serious.

Table 1–3
Number of Major Crimes Committed in the City of Cleveland and Rates per 100,000 Residents, 1965–1974

	1965	1970	1974
Murder			
Number	108	271	298
Rate/100,000	(13.3)	(36.1)	(42.5)
Rape and assault with intent to rape			
Number	149	307	427
Rate/100,000	(18.4)	(40.9)	(60.9)
Robbery and assault with intent to rob			
Number	1832	5475	6066
Rate/100,000	(226.0)	(729.0)	(865.5)
Assault			
Number	3231	5124	5355
Rate/100,000	(398.6)	(682.3)	(761.2)
Breaking and entering			
Number	7374	10,765	12,759
Rate/100,000	(909.7)	(1433.4)	(1820.4)
Larceny			
Number	13,018	18,546	15,607
Rate/100,000	(1606.0)	(2469.5)	(2226.7)
Auto theft			
Number	4921	19,603	13,405
Rate/100,000	(607.1)	(2610.3)	(1912.5)

Source: Cleveland Division of Police Annual Reports.

As is again true of most large cities, there are vastly different probabilities that residents of specific areas of Cleveland will become crime victims. The all-white West Side, for example, has much lower crime rates than the East Side. In 1974, as shown in Table 1–4, an East Side resident would have been three times as likely to be a victim of a major crime (murder, rape, robbery, or assault against his or her person) as a resident of the West Side. An East Sider would have been twice as likely as a West Sider to be a victim of a major crime against property (breaking and entering, larceny, or auto theft). The threat of crime was real in both areas, however.

Within the East Side of Cleveland, crime is much higher in the oldest, poorest, black neighborhoods than elsewhere. The 1974 murder rate for the very deteriorated West Central area, for example, was 250 per 100,000 persons, or four times the rate for the whole East Side and six times the citywide rate of 42.5 per 100,000 residents. In other inner-city East Side areas, the murder rates were also very high (e.g., West Hough, 172.4; East Hough, 105.6; East Central, 116.6; and Kinsman, 186.3). Rates for assault and robbery were also significantly higher in these areas than in other parts of the city. Not surprisingly the rates of population

Table 1–4
Number of Major Crimes Committed in Cleveland's East and West Sides in 1974

	East Side	West Side	City Total
Murder			
Number	276	22	298
Rate/100,000	(63.8)	(8.2)	(42.5)
Rape and assault with intent to rape			
Number	361	66	427
Rate/100,000	(83.4)	(24.6)	(60.9)
Robbery and assault with intent to rob			
Number	5268	798	6066
Rate/100,000	(1217.0)	(297.7)	(865.5)
Assault			
Number	4223	1132	5355
Rate/100,000	(975.6)	(422.3)	(761.2)
Breaking and entering			
Number	9378	3381	12,759
Rate/100,000	(2166.5)	(1261.4)	(1820.4)
Larceny			
Number	11,865	3742	15,607
Rate/100,000	(2741.0)	(1396.1)	(2226.7)
Auto theft			
Number	10,546	2859	13,405
Rate/100,000	(2436.3)	(1066.7)	(1912.5)

Source: Cleveland Division of Police Annual Reports.

loss, property abandonment, poverty, unemployment, and tax delinquency in these neighborhoods were also among the highest in the city.

Housing

Cleveland's population trends have had a devastating impact on the city's
housing stock. The group of potential housing consumers within the city
boundaries is becoming smaller and poorer, which is leading to steady
deterioration of both residential neighborhoods and the structures within
them. As middle- and upper-income families leave the city, their housing
becomes available to lower-income households. Through this "filtering
down," the poorest families can eventually move out of the oldest slums
into areas vacated by those households immediately above them on the
economic ladder. This succession of moves tends to improve the housing
conditions of the poor in the short run. However, if the households
moving into a neighborhood cannot pay enough to support and maintain
the housing in the area, the physical and environmental character of the
neighborhood soon becomes very similar to what was left behind. This
has been the pattern of change in Cleveland.

The landlords in neighborhoods to which the poor are moving typically respond by reducing the amount of maintenance provided to their
buildings. This does not necessarily mean that the landlords are "milk-
ing" the properties. It may simply reflect the fact that the revenues
received from the buildings are no longer sufficient to cover the costs of
operating them well and maintaining them in good condition. Reduced
maintenance eventually leads to deterioration. As buildings deteriorate
and become less desirable, they produce even lower revenues, and landlords are forced to make further maintenance cuts to avoid losses.

Abandonment is the end product of this process. When the minimum
costs of operation exceed revenues, and there is no likely purchaser for
the uneconomic building, the owner simply walks away from the property. In other cases buildings become vacant and are then vandalized.
Rehabilitation costs usually exceed the building values. In the early and
mid-1960s, abandonment was confined to the most dilapidated housing in
Cleveland's worst areas. By 1975, however, structures were being abandoned in nearly all neighborhoods of the East Side and a few sections of
the West Side. In 1974 alone, the Cleveland Bureau of Demolition razed
over 4000 housing units, most of which had been abandoned when they
were condemned. This amounted to more than 1.6 percent of the city's
total housing stock.

Increased demolition has improved Cleveland's inner-city neighborhoods significantly. The removal of hazardous buildings increases open
space, reduces nearby residents' fear of fire and personal violence from

within vacant buildings, and improves perceptions of the neighborhoods by eliminating the worst visible blight. To this end the city has accelerated its demolition activities. Between 1966 and early 1974 the city spent at least $4 million on demolition, and the workload in 1974 exceeded the combined volume of the prior four years. Although demolition is legally the responsibility of the property owner, most of the owners refuse to pay the city. As a result, a high proportion of the demolition costs simply become additional tax liens. Demolition expenditures by the city of Cleveland from 1966 to early 1974 were as follows:

1966–1973 $1.6 million   (Under federal categorical grants, where the federal government paid two-thirds of the contract costs.
The city paid the remaining one-third and all administrative costs.)

1973 $1.5 million   (General revenue sharing funds; $1.3 million in contract costs, $0.2 million for administration.)

1974 $1.0 million   (General revenue sharing funds.)

$0.2 million   (Model Cities funds.)

Many of these demolition expenditures become special assessment liens because property owners do not reimburse the city. As of 1974, some of these liens had not yet been certified over to the Cuyahoga County Auditor.

Cleveland's housing problem is basically an economic problem rooted in three chronic conditions: poverty, the city's declining population, and increases in housing operating cost. According to the 1970 Census, nearly one out of every six Cleveland households had an annual income below $2000. Households with such low incomes cannot possibly pay rents high enough to support housing being maintained in standard condition. The city's population decline means fewer potential occupants for housing, fewer opportunities for landlords to balance revenues from middle-income buildings against losses from low-income buildings, and higher vacancy rates. Rising vacancies further reduce income from rental buildings, especially in the inner city where vacancy rates in excess of 20 percent are not uncommon. Moreover, while revenues from residential properties have been static or declining in many areas, operating costs have risen rapidly. In Cleveland's public housing projects, for example, the average per-unit operating cost rose approximately 70 percent between 1970 and 1974.

Given the unfavorable economics of inner-city rental housing and the rising crime rates in these areas, it is not surprising that some of Cleveland's neighborhoods are declining. Property-owners are allowing their buildings to deteriorate because they foresee no opportunities to derive long-term benefits from maintaining them. If a building or a parcel of land shows no prospect of producing revenue from rent or sale, the owner has little incentive to invest further in the property, or to pay taxes on it.

The bulk of Cleveland's housing deterioration is concentrated in the East Side. The West Side has a basically stable housing market, and considerable rehabilitation has occurred in the innermost area across the Cuyahoga River from downtown. Residential and commercial rehabilitation has been focused in the Ohio City area, but it is expanding, in part through the Neighborhood Housing Services program and the loans made available from Community Development Block Grant funds.

Municipal Finances

Cleveland's tax base has not been expanding, despite considerable redevelopment downtown. In fact, the total assessed valuation of property in the city has been declining in both current and constant dollars. As illustrated in Figure 1–1, the assessed value of real property in Cleveland dropped by 14.8 percent between 1960 and 1974. Over the same period, the real-property assessed valuation in the suburban portion of Cuyahoga County rose by 70.3 percent.

The two primary sources of local revenues in Cleveland are the municipal income tax and the tax on real, utility, and tangible property. The income tax—1 percent of all wages and salaries paid by firms located in Cleveland—is much more productive than the property tax. Despite increases in income tax revenues, however, the city's General Fund was smaller in 1974 than it was in 1969. As shown in Table 1–5, this decrease resulted from a $17.5-million drop in property tax revenues that in turn resulted from failure to renew a property tax levy in 1970. After adjustment for inflation, the decline in General Fund revenues is much sharper. Measured in constant dollars, Cleveland's General Fund revenues dropped by 27 percent between 1969 and 1974.

Cleveland's fiscal problems have been compounded by a 1968 amendment to the City Charter requiring that the city's safety forces (police and fire personnel) be paid 3 percent more than the safety forces in any other Ohio city with a population of over 50,000 persons. As a result of this provision, the Safety Department's total expenditures rose from $42.7 million in 1968 to an estimated $81 million in 1975. Because General Fund revenues declined between 1968 and 1975, other city services had to be cut back substantially.

New sources of revenue have temporarily mitigated Cleveland's financial difficulties. Federal funds for public service employment and General Revenue Sharing bolstered the income side of the city's budget. Also, sale of the municipal sewer system to a regional authority generated

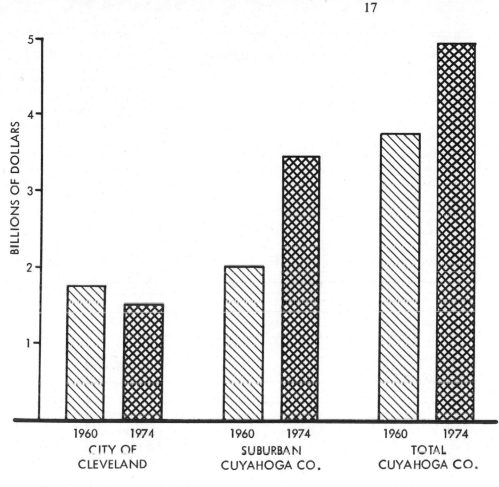

Source: Cuyahoga County Auditor

Figure 1–1. Change in Assessed Valuation of Real Property—City of Cleveland, Suburban County Area, and Cuyahoga County, 1960 and 1974.

$32 million, which was used to continue basic city services. The sale of a city asset produces a one-time gain and is therefore of short-term rather than long-term assistance. Unless the city can attract investments and jobs within its boundaries, its financial future will continue to be clouded.

The Extent of Cleveland's Tax Delinquency

Escalation of tax delinquency in Cleveland has contributed to the city's revenue decline. Table 1–6 illustrates both the magnitude of the delin-

Table 1–5
Local Taxes and Total General Fund Operating Revenues for the City of Cleveland, 1969–1974
(millions of dollars)

Year	Real and Utility Property Tax[a]	Personal Property Tax	Income Tax[b]	Total General Fund Revenues	General Fund in 1974 Constant Dollars
1969	$26,282	$15,171	$35,502	$101,679	$136,299
1970	25,584	15,209	40,639	105,396	133,244
1971	14,271	9,054	37,247	84,545	102,455
1972	14,526	8,455	47,264	94,145	110,499
1973	14,269	8,245	44,841	95,520	105,547
1974	14,379	8,287	50,239	99,599	99,599

Source: Cleveland City Planning Commission.

[a]Property tax revenues dropped sharply after 1970 because a general property tax levy was not renewed.

[b]Prior to 1972 the city returned 25 percent of the income taxes collected from suburban commuters to the municipalities in which they lived, and the suburban municipalities returned 25 percent of the taxes collected from Cleveland residents. This practice was discontinued in 1972. Consequently, city income tax revenues increased substantially in 1972.

quency problem and its startling rate of growth between 1966 and 1974. The number of delinquent parcels increased by 37 percent, and the amount of delinquent taxes rose by over 300 percent. The phenomenal increase in delinquent taxes is due primarily to the bankruptcy of the Penn Central Transportation Company, which, along with several of its subsidiaries, owed approximately $10 million of the almost $23 million in

Table 1–6
Real and Public Utility Tax Delinquency in the City of Cleveland, 1966–1974

Tax Year	Number of Delinquent Parcels	Dollar Value of Delinquent Taxes and Special Assessments	Dollar Value of Delinquent Taxes and Special Assessments, Excluding Railroad Delinquencies[a]
1966	8,213	$5.4 million	$5.4 million
1970	9,003	$10.0 million	$9.5 million
1972	9,971	$16.0 million	$10.8 million
1974	11,286	$22.7 million	$12.6 million

Source: Cuyahoga County Auditor's Billing Tapes for Real and Public Utility Property.

Note: All figures are for the opening of the tax year, even though the actual taxes are not paid until the end of that tax year and the middle of the next. Taxes due for the 1974 tax year, for example, are collected in December 1974 and June 1975.

[a]Most of the parcels owned by the Penn Central Transportation Company and its subsidiaries were certified delinquent in 1971, indicating that they became delinquent in 1970.

delinquent property taxes in 1974.[c] The federal court overseeing the bankruptcy proceedings would not allow payment of any current or delinquent local property taxes. Most of the Penn Central properties in Cleveland were certified delinquent in 1971, and they will continue to accumulate a large, unpaid tax bill until the reorganization of the railroad is complete. It is not known whether those back taxes will ever be paid.

The amount of taxes due on all delinquent property, excluding the Penn Central railroad property, increased from $5.4 million in 1966 to $12.6 million in 1974. Delinquent taxes were rising at a faster rate prior to 1970. From 1966 to 1970, the amount of delinquent taxes increased by $4.1 million, whereas the total rose by only $3.1 million from 1970 to 1974. In contrast, the growth in the number of delinquent parcels between 1970 and 1974 was almost three times that of the previous four-year period. Between 1966 and 1970, the number of delinquent parcels increased by 790; the corresponding rise between 1970 and 1974 was almost 2300 parcels. If this rate of increase were to continue, the dimensions of the delinquency problem would soon be staggering. Assuming that three times as many parcels become delinquent between 1974 and 1978 as between 1970 and 1974, almost 18,000 parcels (over 10 percent of the city total) would be delinquent by 1978.

A number of factors could have contributed to the decreasing rate of growth in the early seventies in the dollar amount of delinquent taxes due. The assessed valuation of property in many areas of the city was reduced in the 1970 countywide reappraisal. Although the tax rate increased by over 30 percent between 1966 and 1974,[d] the aggregate decline in assessed valuation might have been greater for some areas of the city and some types of properties. Those areas and properties might have accounted for a high proportion of the new tax delinquencies. Large sections of Cleveland's East Side, for example, experienced particularly rapid deterioration between 1966 and 1970. Also, more and more of the newly delinquent parcels have been vacant and thus have had lower assessed valuations, on average, than improved parcels. The amount of delinquent taxes that would accumulate on vacant land over time would also be lower than on higher priced, improved parcels.

---

[c]Many of the railroad properties are aggregated into larger parcels for taxing purposes, so less than 30 railroad parcels are delinquent. There are over 11,000 delinquent parcels in the city. Consequently, the railroad delinquencies have not significantly influenced the increase in the number of delinquent parcels. At the end of the 1974 tax year, the state of Ohio reimbursed the county for approximately $519,000 in property tax rollbacks for past years on delinquent parcels. The state now pays 10 percent of the taxes due on *all* parcels. This 10 percent is called the state "rollback." The settlement for the rollback on delinquent parcels is now made annually. The delinquent rollback on railroad property amounted to $273,000 of the $519,000 paid in 1975.

[d]The property tax rate in Cleveland increased from 52.9 mills in the 1966 tax year to 69 mills in the 1974 tax year.

Despite these possible explanations for lower per-parcel taxes, the rapid increase in the number of delinquent parcels after 1970 should have had at least a partially offsetting effect. Delinquent general taxes, special assessments, and penalties levied for nonpayment are all included in delinquent tax liens. Thus the dollar figures for 1972 and 1974 reflect the city's more aggressive actions in demolishing condemned structures. If the owner of a condemned building fails to rehabilitate or raze it within a specified period, the city demolishes the structure to protect the "public's health and safety." As mentioned earlier, demolition expenditures are certified to the Cuyahoga County Auditor as special assessment liens against the property if the owner fails to reimburse the city.

In 1973, the City Planning Commission estimated that demolition of all vacant buildings in Cleveland that were then condemnable would require approximately $2.5 million. At that time the commission also estimated that 800 to 1200 structures would be abandoned each year. Prompt demolition of buildings as they were abandoned would require an expenditure of from $1.3 to $1.9 million annually.[5] If the city's demolition program were to keep pace with the rate of abandonment, the dollar volume of delinquent special assessments would rise substantially since prior experience indicates that only a small proportion of the owners of abandoned structures actually pay the city's bills for demolition.

Geographic Areas of Concentrated Delinquency

Tax delinquent real property appears most frequently in those parts of the city that are badly deteriorated. In these areas, land has lost what is usually considered to be its intrinsic value, and owners have found it difficult—and even impossible—to maintain their properties profitably. The market for land and buildings has weakened progressively, and has collapsed in some areas.

The delinquency problem is more severe on the city's East Side than on the somewhat more affluent West Side. In 1974, only 7 percent of Cleveland's dollar volume of delinquent taxes was due on properties located on the West Side, but 48 percent was due on East Side properties. The remaining 45 percent was owed on railroad property. Over 27 percent of the city's dollar volume of delinquent taxes was due on property located in six East Side statistical areas. Five of these six areas have experienced very serious deterioration, and the sixth, Glenville, is in the middle of the process of neighborhood decline. The geographic concentration of delinquent tax dollars is summarized in Table 1–7. Back in 1966, the delinquency problem was also focused on the city's East Side. At that time over four-fifths of the delinquent taxes were due on property located east of the Cuyahoga River.

Table 1–7
Geographic Distribution of Delinquent Property Tax Dollars in the City of Cleveland in 1974

	% of Total Delinquent Property Tax Dollars in the City of Cleveland
Railroads	45%
West Side	7%
East Side	48%
Selected East Side Statistical Areas	
Glenville	5.2%
West Hough	6.5
East Hough	3.6
East Central	4.7
West Central	5.7
Kinsman[a]	1.7
Total in 6 Areas	27.4%

Source: 1974 Cuyahoga County Auditor's Billing Tape.

[a]The Kinsman area does not account for a very significant portion of the delinquent taxes in the city, but it is included here because the incidence of tax delinquency in the area is high. In comparison with other statistical areas, Kinsman has a relatively small number of parcels.

The distribution of delinquent parcels is similar to that of delinquent tax dollars and also reflects heavy, and increasing, concentration on the East Side. As shown in Table 1–8, 81 percent of the delinquent parcels in 1974 were on the East Side, as compared to 75 percent in 1966. Over 47 percent of the parcels delinquent in 1974 were located in the same six East Side statistical areas discussed previously, although those areas contained only 14 percent of the total real estate parcels in the city.

As suggested by Table 1–8, most of the growth in tax delinquency between 1966 and 1974 occurred on the East Side. In 1974 Cleveland had 3073 more delinquent parcels than in 1966. The number of delinquent parcels on the West Side remained almost constant, as shown in Table 1–9, but an additional 2975 parcels became delinquent on the East Side during this period. Two-thirds of the increase in the number of delinquent parcels in the city was concentrated in the six East Side statistical areas that had the highest delinquency rates.

In the city's stable neighborhoods—those where the housing market appears to be healthy and incomes of residents are relatively high—only 1 percent to 3 percent of the properties are delinquent. This can be considered Cleveland's "normal" delinquency rate. In the city as a whole, 6.5 percent of the parcels were delinquent in 1974. In the most deteriorated areas, the proportion of delinquent parcels is much higher than in the more stable neighborhoods. In West Hough, over 30 percent of the

Table 1–8
Location of Delinquent Parcels in the City of Cleveland, 1966 and 1974

	% of City's Delinquent Parcels[a]		% of Total Parcels in the City[b]	
	1966	1974	1966	1974
East Side	75%	81%	58%	57%
Selected East Side Statistical Areas				
Glenville	7.4%	9.8%	4.4%	4.3%
West Hough	5.7	9.0	1.9	1.8
East Hough	4.2	6.8	2.2	2.1
East Central	8.8	9.6	2.8	2.8
West Central	11.2	8.8	2.7	2.4
Kinsman	2.5	3.2	0.9	0.9
Total in 6 Areas	39.8%	47.2%	14.9%	14.3%
West Side	25%	19%	42%	43%

Source: Cuyahoga County Auditor's Billing Tapes.
[a] Delinquent railroad parcels are included, but they account for such a small portion of the total number of delinquent parcels that they do not affect percentages appreciably.
[b] The percent of total parcels in the city changed slightly between 1966 and 1974 due to the merging and splitting of parcels as ownership changed.

parcels were delinquent in 1974. In several other areas, as shown in Table 1–10, at least 20 percent of the parcels were delinquent in 1974.

Delinquency has increased rapidly in East and West Hough, reflecting the severe decline in those areas. The percentage of parcels delinquent in both areas more than doubled between 1966 and 1974. The Hough riots, which occurred in 1966, undoubtedly had an adverse effect on people's confidence in the desirability of property ownership in the area. In the late 1960s and early 1970s, delinquency in the West Central area increased much less quickly than in Hough, but the delinquency problem was already more advanced in West Central in 1966. A substantial amount of

Table 1–9
Number of Delinquent Parcels in the City of Cleveland, 1966–1974

Year	City Total	East Side	West Side
1966	8,213	6,174	2,039
1970	9,003	7,025	1,978
1972	9,971	7,806	2,165
1974	11,286	9,149	2,137
Increase, 1966–1974	3,073	2,975	98

Source: Cuyahoga County Auditor's Data.

Table 1-10
Delinquency Rates in Central East Side Statistical Areas of Cleveland, 1966-1974

Statistical Area		Delinquent Parcels as % of Total Properties	
Number	Name	1966	1974
5	Glenville	7.9%	14.5%
8	West Hough	14.4	32.0
9	East Hough	8.7	21.0
11	East Central	14.5	21.9
12	West Central	19.6	23.4
13	Kinsman	12.5	22.7

Source: Cuyahoga County Auditor's Billing Tapes.

public redevelopment has taken place in West Central, so a number of parcels that were or would have become delinquent are now under public or nonprofit ownership. In Glenville, where the housing market is weakening, delinquency is rising rapidly. Examination of delinquency rates in the neighborhoods adjacent to the East Side areas that currently have high delinquency levels indicates that the problem is spreading. The three maps in Figure 1-2, which depict the increase in delinquency since 1966 by statistical area, clearly illustrate that much of the East Side was experiencing high rates of property tax delinquency by 1974.

South Collinwood, Forest Hills, Norwood, University Circle, Woodland Hills, Paul Revere, Mount Pleasant, and Miles-Warner all appear to be in the initial stages of a delinquency problem. Delinquency rates in these areas ranged from 5.2 percent in South Collinwood to 8.3 percent in Norwood in 1974. Previous City Planning Commission studies indicated that the housing markets in these areas had begun to weaken, and the emergence of higher-than-normal property tax delinquency confirms that analysis. Table 1-11 summarizes the growth of the delinquency problem in these East Side areas from 1966 to 1974. The delinquency rate in the Lee-Seville-Miles area is exceptionally high.

Three West Side areas—the Near West Side, Tremont, and Fulton-Train—also exhibit the beginnings of abnormal delinquency. These three areas have the weakest housing markets on the West Side. A 1973 City Planning Commission study compared the housing markets in these areas to those in Norwood, Goodrich, and Forest Hills on the East Side.[6] As can be seen by comparing the figures in Table 1-12 with those in Table 1-11, their patterns of tax delinquency are also similar. The 1974 delinquency rates in the three West Side areas ranged from 5.5 percent in Fulton-Train to 7.8 percent in Tremont. Some of the incidents of tax

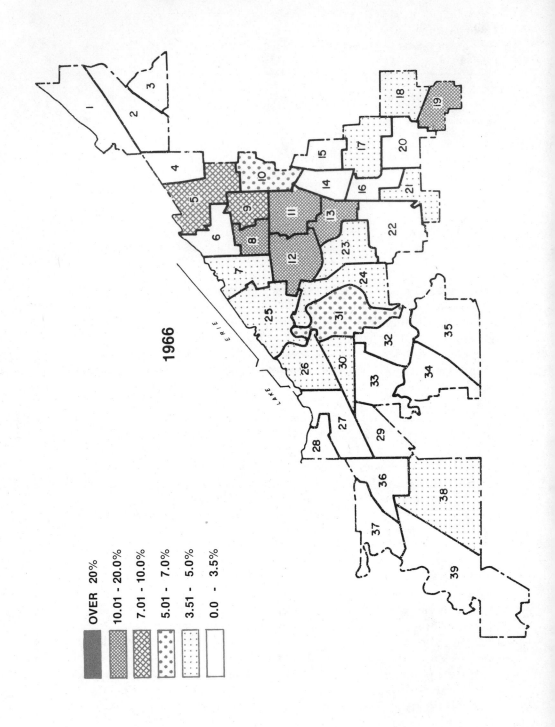

1966

LAKE ERIE

OVER 20%

10.01 - 20.0%

7.01 - 10.0%

5.01 - 7.0%

3.51 - 5.0%

0.0 - 3.5%

25

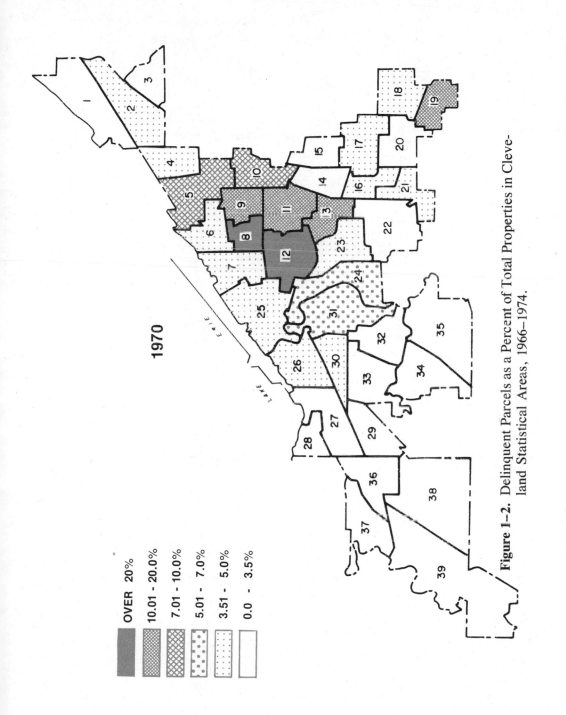

Figure 1–2. Delinquent Parcels as a Percent of Total Properties in Cleveland Statistical Areas, 1966–1974.

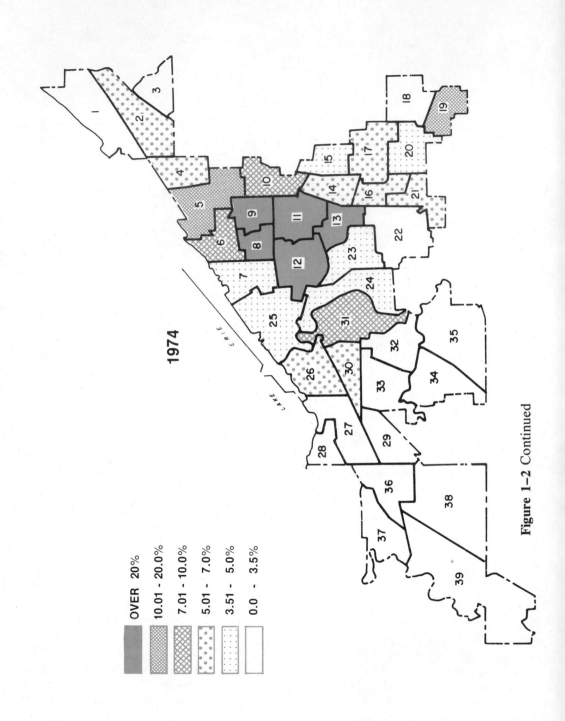

1974

OVER 20%
10.01 - 20.0%
7.01 - 10.0%
5.01 - 7.0%
3.51 - 5.0%
0.0 - 3.5%

Figure 1-2 Continued

Table 1–11
Delinquency Rates in Peripheral Statistical Areas of Cleveland's East Side,
1966–1974

Statistical Area		Delinquent Parcels as % of Total Properties			% Increase (Decrease) in Number of Delinquent Parcels,
Number	Name	1966	1970	1974	1966–1974
2	South Collinwood	3.3%	3.8%	5.2%	55%
4	Forest Hills	2.8	4.0	6.7	136
6	Norwood	2.8	3.7	8.3	198
10	University Circle	6.3	7.2	7.2	12
14	Woodland Hills	2.6	2.9	5.4	102
16	Paul Revere	2.7	4.1	5.7	111
17	Mount Pleasant	4.7	4.6	5.9	27
19	Lee-Seville-Miles	15.0	12.8	13.0	(17)
21	Miles-Warner	3.5	4.1	5.8	64

Source: Cuyahoga County Auditor's Billing Tapes.

delinquency in Fulton-Train are related to land acquisition for Interstate-90, which is planned to go through the area, but that accounts for only part of what is clearly a larger problem.

Value of Tax Delinquent Parcels

For tax purposes real property in Cleveland is valued at approximately one-third its market value, or probable cash selling price in a normal, open market. The tax value of a property is known as its assessed valuation. A reappraisal of Cuyahoga County real estate for tax purposes was underway in 1975 and became effective in 1976. Thus our 1974 and earlier data reflect the preceding countywide assessment, which took place in 1970.

Only a small proportion of the delinquent parcels in the city of Cleveland had extremely low assessed valuations in 1974. Among the total parcels on which delinquent taxes were due, less than 13 percent had assessed valuations of $1000 or less (or approximate market values of $3000 or less). Only 5 percent of the properties had assessed values of $500 or less. In contrast, almost 60 percent had 1974 assessed values falling between $2001 and $7500, which suggest market values of between $6000 and $22,500. As shown in Table 1–13, 72 percent of the nondelinquent parcels in Cleveland fell within the latter assessed value range, so there was not a marked difference between the values of delinquent and

Table 1–12
Delinquency Rates in Selected West Side Statistical Areas, 1966–1974

Statistical Area		Delinquent Parcels as % of Total Properties			% Increase in Number of Delinquent Parcels, 1966–1974
Number	Name	1966	1970	1974	
26	Near West Side	4.7%	4.7%	6.1%	29%
30	Fulton-Train	3.9	4.2	5.5	39
31	Tremont	6.2	6.0	7.8	26

Source: Cuyahoga County Auditor's Billing Tapes.

nondelinquent parcels in the city in 1974. Not surprisingly, the assessed valuations of delinquent properties in the six East Side statistical areas where delinquency is more concentrated are lower than the valuations in the city as a whole. Though delinquent parcels in those areas tend to have lower valuations than nondelinquent parcels, many of the delinquent properties have values typical of large numbers of other nondelinquent properties.

In 1966 a higher proportion of delinquent parcels in Cleveland had low values. At that time over 17 percent of the tax delinquent properties in the city were valued at $1000 or less, as compared to 13 percent of the parcels in 1974. The increase in delinquency among properties with higher valuations becomes particularly clear in an examination of delinquent vacant land. In 1974 only 15 percent of the vacant parcels that were delinquent had assessed values of $500 or less, whereas in 1966, 45 percent of the vacant delinquent parcels were valued at $500 or less. The rise in delinquency among higher value parcels that has occurred in Cleveland since 1966 reflects the weakening of the land market in many areas of the city.

An increasing proportion of the delinquent parcels in Cleveland are vacant, which is a result of the extensive abandonment and demolition that have occurred in many of the city's neighborhoods. Because the reuse of this land is not financially feasible, it simply lies vacant and property taxes are not paid. In 1966 only 21 percent of the tax delinquent parcels were vacant. By the time of our field survey in 1975, 40 percent of the city's delinquent properties were vacant. As we will discuss in more detail in Chapters 5 and 6, the incidence of delinquent vacant land is especially high in Hough and West Central. Only 10 percent of the delinquent parcels in West Hough were vacant in 1966, but the figure had risen to 58 percent by 1975.

The longer a parcel has been delinquent, the higher the probability

Table 1–13
Assessed Valuation of Delinquent Property in Cleveland in 1974

Assessed Valuation	% of Total Parcels on 1974 Duplicate							
	$0[a]	$1–$350	$351–$500	$501–$1000	$1601–$2000	$2001–$5000	$5001–$7500	$7501 +
Delinquent parcels	0.6%	3.3%	1.3%	7.6%	20.1%	42.1%	16.2%	8.8%
(Cumulative total)	—	3.9	5.2	12.8	32.9	75.0	91.2	100.0
Nondelinquent parcels	7.4	0.3	0.2	0.9	3.8	33.2	38.7	15.5
(Cumulative total)	—	7.7	7.9	8.8	12.6	45.8	84.5	100.0

Source: Cuyahoga County Auditor's 1974 Billing Tape.

[a]Tax-exempt properties. Some parcels had delinquent taxes owing at the time the exemption was granted.

that it will be vacant. As owner interest in a property wanes, management functions are neglected or purposely stopped. Then vacancy rises. After the last tenant leaves, the structure is often vandalized, condemned, and demolished. In such a case, tax delinquency is simply a symptom of an increasingly nonviable real estate market and it is a precursor of abandonment. Although this situation is typical in Cleveland and accounts for a very large share of the tax delinquency (as discussed in later chapters), it is by no means the only scenario for delinquent parcels. Some owners are tax delinquent in order to reduce their holding costs on properties that they plan to sell; then they pay back taxes at the time of sale. Other owners suffer temporary, or what they think will be temporary, financial difficulties and therefore postpone tax payment in anticipation of better times. Often their tax bills accumulate for several years and become an impossible financial burden. In a declining real estate market, the aggregate delinquent taxes may actually exceed the value of the property. If foreclosure occurs on such properties, the owners may lose their entire investments.

Many questions remain to be answered about the nature of the tax delinquency problem before policy recommendations can be made. A shorter foreclosure process might increase the rate of abandonment, as property owners find redemption financially infeasible. Changes in the foreclosure procedure might also radically alter the scope of the city's management and maintenance responsibilities. In short, policies and programs that fail to recognize the basic realities of the city's land and housing markets may only exacerbate the situation.

The questions considered in the Cleveland study are those that will be asked by other cities facing rising tax delinquency. Cleveland's delinquency problem is certainly not unique, though its magnitude may be greater than in most cities. In addition to the tax issues, our analysis provides insight into the difficulties inherent in any sort of government intervention or regulation in the private low-income housing market. Among the questions we will address in subsequent chapters are the following:

1. How well does the current foreclosure process in Cleveland—and throughout most of the United States—serve the needs of taxing jurisdictions and protect property owners? (Chapter 2)
2. Is Missouri's legislation, which enables rapid foreclosure and municipal acquisition of delinquent properties, a good model for other states and cities? (Chapter 3)
3. How well does tax delinquency correlate with the decline process in urban neighborhoods? (Chapter 4)
4. What are the physical, ownership, and occupancy characteristics of tax delinquent parcels? (Chapter 5)

5. Is tax delinquency a tactic used by slum landlords to increase their profits? (Chapter 6)
6. What would happen to residents of low-income areas if rapid foreclosure were instituted? (Chapter 6)
7. What can and should be done to reduce the administrative costs and revenue losses resulting from real estate tax delinquency? (Chapter 7)

Notes

1. All figures are taken from William L. C. Wheaton, *Tax Delinquent Lands in Cuyahoga County* Publication no. 13 (Regional Association of Cleveland, October 1941).

2. Thomas S. Andrzejewski, "Delinquent Taxes May Cost County up to $29 Million," *The Plain Dealer*, September 1, 1974, p. 1.

3. ADC caseload figures were provided by the Cleveland Federation for Community Planning.

4. Cleveland City Planning Commission, "Two Percent Household Survey: Results of All Questions," June 1972.

5. Cleveland City Planning Commission, "Cleveland's Abandonment Problem in 1973," May 1974, p. 15.

6. Cleveland City Planning Commission, "Poverty and Substandard Housing," March 1973.

2

**Cleveland's Property
Tax–Foreclosure
Process**

Foreclosure processes are aimed toward recovering delinquent tax revenues and returning properties to taxpaying status. In Cleveland and other central cities, however, recent fundamental changes in the market for inner-city land have significantly reduced the effectiveness of existing foreclosure procedures. The incidence of property tax delinquency has increased substantially in Cleveland, as described in Chapter 1, particularly in those neighborhoods experiencing heavy deterioration, abandonment, and population loss. Property tax delinquency in the city is now a result not only of personal financial difficulties but also of lack of demand for land that has very limited reuse potential.

The sheer volume of the increase in tax delinquency in Cleveland has placed severe pressures on the administrative procedures for tax foreclosure. Moreover, the weakening of the real estate market in many areas of the city has made the recovery of tax delinquent revenues much more difficult. A lack of bidders often results in foreclosed properties not being sold. Purchasers at tax sales are generally willing to pay only a fraction of the former values of the properties. They appear to be purchasing for speculation, not immediate reuse, because the properties frequently become delinquent again shortly after the sales. In many cases the administrative costs incurred in bringing parcels to sale are far greater than the sale revenues.

This chapter summarizes Cuyahoga County's recent experience, in the city of Cleveland, under the existing foreclosure process and identifies the constraints imposed on the administration of the current system by lack of demand for inner-city real estate. Ohio's foreclosure process and the inadequacies of that process for coping with the new type of inner-city tax delinquency are by no means unique. As is discussed in the next chapter, Missouri enacted new legislation in 1971 to assist St. Louis in dealing with the same problem. Representatives from municipalities around the country have visited St. Louis and have attended conferences to discuss the city's new Land Reutilization Authority, presumably because many people are searching for ways to deal with their own municipal tax delinquencies. Pittsburgh, Newark, and other cities have been studying property tax delinquency and searching for remedies. Municipalities with increasing nonpayment of taxes in areas of declining property values need to develop new procedures that will accomplish the following:

1. Enable taxing bodies to obtain compensation for lost tax revenues and property maintenance expenditures.
2. Ease administrative burdens of foreclosure while protecting the rights of owners of delinquent properties.
3. Strengthen disincentives to tax delinquency.
4. Facilitate eventual reuse of inner-city land.

Before new procedures can be devised or evaluated, the current foreclosure process and its inadequacies must be clearly understood. Thus the remainder of this chapter is devoted to a description of the workings of the foreclosure process in Cuyahoga County. Although the specific steps in foreclosure vary from state to state, Ohio's overall process is typical of that followed in most places.

Howard C. Emmerman classifies state tax sale systems into two general types, the two-sale system and the one-sale system. In the two-sale system, a receiver who will earn interest for holding the property acquires it at a preliminary tax lien sale, and the perfected title is transferred at a later tax deed sale. The one-sale system has four sub-classifications:

1. Bid-down system—One sale confers inchoate tax title on the receiver willing to accept the lowest interest prior to possible redemption; title is automatically perfected during the redemption period.
2. Public auction system—The highest cash bidder receives inchoate title along with exclusive right of perfection of the title. This system is followed in Ohio and in twenty other states and the District of Columbia.
3. Tax sale/no bid-down system—The person willing to pay the taxes and costs for the smallest dividend receives inchoate title and the exclusive right to perfection of title.
4. Automatic sale to state system—In eight western states, title automatically transfers to the state at the end of the redemption period; the state may then sell, use, or lease the property.[1]

The Steps in Foreclosure

In Cuyahoga County, as in other taxing jurisdictions, properties are not foreclosed upon immediately after they become delinquent. A period of redemption is allowed, during which an owner is given the opportunity to repay delinquent taxes without being threatened with losing the property. This redemption period evolved to protect property owners who could not pay their taxes because of temporary financial difficulties. Actually, an owner's equity of redemption continues throughout the foreclosure process, until title is transferred to another owner.

Figure 2–1 illustrates the general administrative procedure for foreclosing on tax delinquent properties in Cuyahoga County. The sequencing is dictated by Ohio statutory provisions, though the timing of the various steps in the Ohio code is directive, not mandatory, so long as the minimum specified times are observed. Administrators can lengthen the process, if necessary, without losing the right to foreclose.

As shown in Step 1 in Figure 2–1, a parcel cannot be "certified" delinquent until the taxes have gone unpaid for at least two consecutive semiannual collection periods.[2] At the end of each August settlement, according to the Ohio statute, the county auditor is to certify a list of delinquent properties and send a copy to the county treasurer (Step 2). The statute then directs the auditor to publish the delinquent land list twice, in two separate newspapers, within sixty days (Step 3). At least one year must pass after the property has been certified before the auditor issues a "delinquent land tax certificate" and sends a copy to the county prosecutor (Step 4). The prosecutor is then responsible for initiating foreclosure proceedings (Step 5); the statute states that these proceedings will begin within six months of delivery of the delinquent land tax certificate.

Under the Ohio statute, a parcel remains tax delinquent for a minimum of two years before it can be sold to recover the outstanding taxes. In Cuyahoga County, Steps 1 through 5 have historically taken more than two years. The list of delinquent parcels has usually been advertised about a year after certification, which has cut down the advertising costs because taxes are paid on approximately one-third of the delinquent parcels within the first year after certification and a small number of property owners also make partial payments or enter into contracts to pay their delinquent taxes in installments.[a] Despite these cost savings in extending the process, in 1975 the county auditor was attempting to reduce the elapsed time between certification and advertising. The parcels certified delinquent in 1973 and 1974 on the tax duplicates prepared in December 1973 and December 1974 were advertised in May 1975.

The processing of delinquent parcels in Cuyahoga County is plagued by a number of difficulties that slow it down considerably. The foreclo-

---

[a]Based on an analysis of the Cuyahoga County Delinquent Land Lists for 1972 and 1973. Partial payments were made on the delinquent taxes on 7.6 percent of the parcels on the 1972 Delinquent Land List by the end of the 1972 tax year. The owners of 4 percent of the parcels entered into contracts to pay the delinquent taxes in installments. On the 1973 Delinquent Land List, only 1 percent of the parcels were listed as under contract by the end of the 1973 tax year. No taxes were listed as partially paid.

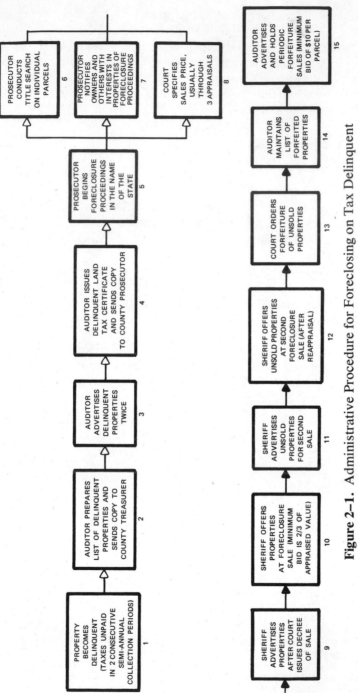

Figure 2–1. Administrative Procedure for Foreclosing on Tax Delinquent Properties in Cuyahoga County.

Note: A tax delinquent parcel is removed from this process if the owner appeals the assessed valuation to the Board of Tax Revision or if the owner enters a contract with the county treasurer's office to pay the delinquent taxes over time. If taxes are not paid after a ruling by the Board of Tax Revision or if the owner defaults on the tax payment contract, the property reenters the foreclosure process.

Source: Cleveland City Planning Commission; *Ohio Revised Code,* Chapters 5721 and 5723.

sure process involves a costly title search and notification procedure (Steps 6 and 7). When the county prosecutor attempts to notify all parties with an interest in each property, the process is hampered by inadequacies in the real property transfer records. For example, state law does not require a property-owner to list an address where he or she can be reached in case of an administrative action concerning the property. A property-owner has the option of providing the county treasurer with an address where he or she wishes the tax bill to be sent, but an owner also has the option of not listing an address and picking up the tax bill at the County Administration Building. Another problem of notification arises when the original owner is deceased; often the heirs are not aware of their ownership or are not interested in the property. As shown in Step 8 in Figure 2–1, property appraisals also must often be performed to serve as a basis for the court's determining the minimum bid for the parcel at the sheriff's sale.[b]

The Tax Division of the Cuyahoga County Prosecutor's Office has not had the staff to handle the massive amount of work generated by the increase in the number of delinquent parcels. Consequently, processing has moved very slowly. Examination of sheriff's sales between 1969 and 1974 revealed that it took approximately ten years for a parcel to reach the point of sale after it had been certified delinquent.

Once the county prosecutor has completed the required preparatory work on a large enough number of tax delinquent properties, a sheriff's sale can be planned. As shown in Step 9, the list of sale properties must first be advertised, and then the sale can be held (Step 10). The minimum bid at the sheriff's sale is two-thirds of a parcel's appraised value, or the total amount of outstanding liens if no special appraisals were done. Properties that are not sold at those prices at one sheriff's sale are offered a second time (Steps 11 and 12), usually after being reappraised at lower values. After two unsuccessful offerings at sheriff's sales, the court orders forfeiture of unsold properties (Step 13), and they are added to the auditor's List of Forfeited Properties (Step 14). After that, they can be offered at auditor's forfeiture sales, where the minimum bid is only $10 per parcel (Step 15).

In 1974 over 60 percent of Cleveland's delinquent parcels were not yet eligible for foreclosure or had only recently been sent to the county prosecutor. Approximately 3500 parcels had been certified delinquent long enough for the preliminary foreclosure steps to have been com-

---

[b]In addition to the delay-causing factors cited in the text, parcels eligible for foreclosure can be temporarily removed from the process if the owner enters into a contract to pay delinquent taxes over a period of time. An owner who has filed an appeal with the Board of Tax Revision contesting a parcel's assessed valuation also will not be foreclosed against. If the owner defaults on the contract or the board upholds the valuation and back taxes are not paid, the county prosecutor then begins foreclosure.

Table 2–1
Length of Delinquency of City of Cleveland Parcels, as of 1974

Tax Year Certified Delinquent	Number of Delinquent Parcels	Percent of Total Delinquent Parcels	Number of Delinquent Parcels on Contract
With outstanding delinquencies but not yet certified delinquent:	2,498	22.1%	11
1974	2,369	21.0	43
1973	1,247	11.0	75
1972	921	8.2	102
Eligible for foreclosure:			
1971	821	7.3	61
1970	679	6.0	47
1969	497	4.4	43
1968	461	4.1	77
1965–1967	981	8.7	232
1962–1964	362		101
1959–1961	170		50
1954–1958	153	7.2	41
1950–1953	61		8
Before 1950	66		9
Total	11,286	100.0%	900

Source: 1974 Cuyahoga County Auditor's Billing Tape.
Note: The parcels certified delinquent in 1971 or earlier could have been brought to sale by 1974 if optimum processing times had been followed.

pleted.[c] As Table 2–1 indicates, many of the parcels had been delinquent for longer than the minimum time specified by the Ohio statute. Actually, only a small portion of the parcels eligible for sale each year are offered at foreclosure or forfeiture sales.[3] As of 1975 there had not been a forfeiture sale in Cuyahoga County since 1972 because the auditor was waiting for enough parcels to move through the various preliminary steps (including two sheriff's sales) to justify holding a sale.

[c]Of the 4251 parcels that were certified delinquent in the 1971 tax year or earlier and that should have been sent to the prosecutor by the 1973 tax year, 669 were listed on the 1974 Cuyahoga County Billing Tape as being under contract to pay the taxes. Therefore a total of 3528 parcels were eligible for sale. There were, however, no available records of the number of delinquent parcels on which Board of Tax Revision complaints had been filed. Some of the 3500 parcels were probably in the appeals process, which would have reduced the number of eligible parcels.

The Ohio statute allows the prosecutor to initiate foreclosure proceedings one year after certification. If the process in Cuyahoga County moved as swiftly as the law allowed, an additional 1991 parcels would have been eligible for foreclosure in 1974. (Parcels certified delinquent in 1972 and 1973, less those on contract.) The severe burden placed on the Cuyahoga County administrative system by the rapid growth in delinquencies in the city of Cleveland makes adherence to the directives in the statute impossible under current funding levels.

Although a tax delinquent property could be brought to sale in Ohio within three years if the statutory process were strictly followed, the actual elapsed time is much longer. A typical time sequence in Cuyahoga County is as follows:

1965—Property becomes delinquent
1967—Property appears in auditor's advertisement
1970—Delinquent land tax certificate goes to prosecutor
1971—Prosecutor files foreclosure action
1973—Court issues decree of sale
1974—Sheriff offers property at foreclosure sale

A nine-year period, in this case, leads to the property's being brought to sale for the first time. If the property does not sell for the full amount of taxes, assessments, costs, and penalties at the first sheriff's sale, it must be offered again. Then it can be sent to forfeiture. Thus another two years could easily be added to the previous nine before the property would be disposed of at a forfeiture sale.

Cuyahoga County's experience with Cleveland properties at tax sales indicates that, if all eligible delinquent parcels were to be offered for sale, the county would obtain only a small portion of the delinquent tax revenues while incurring tremendous administrative costs. In almost every case the administrative costs to bring a delinquent parcel to the point of the final forfeiture sale are greater than the price for which the parcel can be sold.

Several assumptions about the marketability of tax delinquent real property underlie the existing statutory and administrative procedures for tax foreclosure. The process aims at the recovery of delinquent tax revenue and the return of real estate to tax-paying status, which assumes that:

1. Some people are willing to purchase tax delinquent properties offered at sheriff's sales and forfeiture sales.
2. Properties offered at these sales have reasonable market values, so purchasers will be willing to pay enough to allow recovery of most, if not all, of the delinquent taxes and administrative costs incurred in bringing the parcels to sale.
3. Purchasers of sale parcels will be capable of and interested in maintaining their investments in the properties, including paying future property taxes. Thus formerly delinquent land will be productively contributing to the tax rolls again.

We will examine each of these assumptions in turn. Essentially, our findings demonstrate that these assumptions do not accurately reflect the current situation in Cleveland. A procedure requiring the sale of tax delinquent parcels, regardless of the final disposition price, will result in neither the recovery of a substantial portion of the delinquent tax revenue nor the return of the properties to the tax duplicate. The weakness of the real estate market in many Cleveland neighborhoods requires the development of alternative methods of compensating for lost tax revenues.

Results of Recent Tax Sales

When the county prosecutor's work on tax delinquent parcels is completed, the properties are first offered at one or more sheriff's foreclosure sales. Of the 189 tax-foreclosed parcels in the city of Cleveland that were made available at sheriff's sales in Cuyahoga County in 1969, 1970, and 1971, slightly over one-third were sold. The record was worse in 1973 and 1974: only 23 percent of the 198 available Cleveland parcels were sold. The results of individual sales for the six-year period are shown in Table 2–2.

Parcels that the sheriff cannot sell are offered later at an auditor's sale of forfeited property. The sales rates at forfeiture sales are much higher than at sheriff's sales. As Table 2–3 indicates, over 80 percent of the parcels offered in both 1969 and 1972 were sold. The significantly lower prices at the forfeiture sales appear to increase the attractiveness of delinquent property purchases.

The minimum bid at a sheriff's sale the first time a parcel is offered is two-thirds of its appraised value. The minimum bid is usually lowered if

Table 2–2
Disposition of Cleveland Parcels at Sheriff's Sales of Tax-Foreclosed Properties, 1969–1974

		Parcels Sold	
Year	Parcels Offered	Number	%
1969	56	14	25%
1970	83	34	41
1971	50	20	40
Subtotal	189	68	36%
1973	77	14	18%
1974	121	31	26
Subtotal	198	45	23%
Total, '69–74	387	113	29%

Source: Cuyahoga County Sheriff's Lists of Properties Offered at Foreclosure Sales.

Table 2–3
Disposition of Cleveland Parcels at Auditor's Sales of Forfeited Properties, 1969 and 1972

Year	Parcels Offered	Parcels Sold	
		Number	%
1969	236	195	83%
1972	286	242	85
Total	522	437	84%

Source: Cuyahoga County Auditor's Forfeited Land List.

an unsold property is offered again at a subsequent sale. Over one-half of the parcels that were sold at Cuyahoga County sheriff's sales from 1969 to 1971 were purchased for less than $1000. As shown in Table 2–4, almost 40 percent of the parcels disposed of at the 1973 and 1974 Sheriff's sales were sold for less than $1000, and only 4 percent were sold for $5000 or more.

The sales prices of almost 88 percent of the Cleveland parcels purchased at sheriff's sales in 1969, 1970, and 1971 were equal to no more than one-half of the market values indicated by their assessed valuations.[d] The corresponding figure for the 1973 and 1974 sheriff's sales was 84 percent, as indicated in Table 2–5. Despite the relatively low prices obtained for tax delinquent parcels at the sheriff's sales, most of the parcels offered do not sell. The real estate market in many areas of the city of Cleveland is simply not strong enough to make the purchase of delinquent parcels attractive to potential investors, even at two-thirds (or less) of their appraised values.

Only a small investment is needed to purchase a tax delinquent property at the auditor's forfeiture sale; the minimum bid is $10 per parcel. One-third of the city parcels disposed of at the 1969 and 1972 forfeiture sales were sold for $50 or less, as shown in Table 2–6, and nearly two-thirds were sold for $150 or less.

The availability of real estate, much of it vacant land, at such "bar-

[d]In Cuyahoga County, a property's assessed value is approximately one-third its market value. In the 1970 countywide appraisal, market value was determined primarily by the replacement value of the improvements less depreciation, plus the value of the land. This figure gives an approximate indication of the former value of these parcels. Assessed value may indicate a different market value than the appraisal made as part of the foreclosure process. The appraisal made for the sheriff's sale may be lower for a number of reasons. For example, vandals may have severely damaged an abandoned structure, or an owner of an unused building might not have applied for an assessment reduction. If a parcel is not sold the first time it is offered, the court may order that the minimum acceptable bid be reduced for subsequent sales.

Table 2–4

Prices Obtained for Tax Delinquent Cleveland Properties at Sheriff's Sales, 1969–1974

	Number of Parcels Sold		% of Total Parcels Sold	
Sales Price	1969– 1971	1973– 1974[a]	1969– 1971	1973– 1974
Less than $500	19	8	28%	19%
$500–$999	16	8	24	19
$1000–$4999	26	25	38	58
$5000–$10,000	7	0	10	0
Over $10,000	0	2	0	4
Total	68	43	100%	100%

Source: Cuyahoga County Sheriff's Lists of Properties Offered at Foreclosure Sales.
[a] Information not available for two parcels sold.

Table 2–5

Sales-to-Market-Value Ratios for Cleveland Properties Sold at Sheriff's Sales, 1969–1974

	Sales Price as % of Market Value[a]					
Year	Under 10%	10–25%	26–50%	51–75%	76–90%	91% and over
1969	1	5	4	1	1	—
1970	4	15	10	3	—	1
1971	6	11	1	1	1	—
Total	11	31	15	5	2	1
% of total parcels sold in 1969–1971	16.9%	47.7%	23.1%	7.7%	3.1%	1.5%
1973	2	4	6	2	—	—
1974	9	12	3	—	5	—
Total	11	16	9	2	5	—
% of total parcels sold in 1973–1974	25.6%	37.2%	20.9%	4.7%	11.6%	—

Source: Cuyahoga County Sheriff's Lists of Properties Offered at Foreclosure Sales, and Cuyahoga County Auditor's Tax Duplicates of Real and Public Utility Property for years of sales.

[a] Market values were calculated as three times the assessed valuations of individual properties. Information was not available for three of the sixty-eight parcels sold between 1969 and 1971 and for two of the parcels sold in 1973 and 1974.

Table 2–6
Prices Paid for Cleveland Parcels at 1969 and 1972 Forfeiture Sales

Purchase Price	Number Sold[a]	% of Total Sold
$0–$50	144	33.5%
$51–$150	125	29.1
$151–$250	58	13.5
$251–$500	81	18.8
Over $500	22	5.1
Total	430	100.0%

Source: Cuyahoga County Auditor's Forfeited Land List.
[a]Information not available for seven parcels.

gain basement" prices has attracted speculators' interest. As would be expected, the sales prices at forfeiture sales represent much lower proportions of the properties' market values (as indicated by assessed valuations) than at the sheriff's sales. As Table 2–7 indicates, one-half of the Cleveland parcels were purchased in 1969 and 1972 for 5 percent or less of their "market values." Almost three-fourths sold for 10 percent or less of their "market values." By the time a property has been in the foreclosure process long enough to reach a forfeiture sale, its assessed-to-market-value ratio is likely to be well above the countywide goal, which varied during the time of the study from about 28 percent to 33 percent. This assumption is borne out by the figures in Table 2–7.

Table 2–7
Sales-to-Market-Value Ratios for Cleveland Properties Sold at 1969 and 1972 Forfeiture Sales

Purchase Price As % of Market Value[a]	Number of Parcels[b]	% of Total Parcels Sold
1–5%	223	52.2%
5–10%	89	20.8
10–20%	77	18.1
20–30%	26	6.1
Over 30%	12	2.8
	427	100.0%

Source: Cuyahoga County Auditor's Forfeited Land List, and Cuyahoga County Auditor's Tax Duplicates of Real and Public Utility Property for years of sales.
[a]Market values were calculated as three times the assessed valuations of individual properties.
[b]Information was not available for ten parcels.

Sale Revenues in Relation to Costs

The purpose of the tax sale procedure is to recover delinquent tax revenues and to return foreclosed properties to tax-paying status. The very
low prices obtained for Cleveland parcels at tax sales are insufficient to
cover both the delinquent taxes and the administrative costs of the sales.
When the sales price of a tax delinquent parcel does not cover the
outstanding liens against the parcel, the remaining taxes are abated, and
the new owner is not required to make up the difference. Because of the
low tax sale prices, the dollar volume of delinquent taxes being abated is
becoming significant. If the sales price is greater than the amount of
delinquent taxes and administrative costs, the excess is returned to the
owner or to holders of other liens against the property. Thus the taxing
bodies do not even have an opportunity to average their gains and losses.

Substantial, and increasing, administrative costs are incurred by the
county before a parcel can be offered at tax sales. The quantifiable
administrative costs for parcels that sold at sheriff's sales rose from an
average of $331 per parcel in 1969 to $437 per parcel in 1971. The costs
declined slightly in 1973 and 1974, averaging $433 and $389 per parcel,
respectively. This was mainly because fewer parcels were alias and
pluries sales, or parcels that were sold at the second or third offering.
Parcels were sold more frequently on their first offering. If a parcel is not
sold at a sheriff's sale, additional administrative costs are incurred before
it can be offered at the auditor's forfeiture sale because a number of the
administrative steps, such as advertising, must be repeated.

Table 2–8 details the costs of various components of the sale procedure. These figures do not include the time spent by the staffs of the
various county departments (for example, the auditor's, treasurer's, and
prosecutor's offices) involved in processing delinquent properties. Thus
the figures in Table 2–8 represent only a fraction of the true administrative costs. Comparison of the per-parcel quantifiable administrative costs
with the sales prices of parcels at the tax sales indicates that in some
cases, particularly at the forfeiture sale, the monies received are not
adequate to cover even these partial costs. Only 5 percent of the parcels
sold at the forfeiture sales in 1969 and 1972 produced more than $500
each.

Neither the sheriff's nor the auditor's sales have generated enough
revenue to offset administrative costs and delinquent taxes due. The
properties sold at sheriff's sales in 1969, 1970, and 1971 had accumulated
delinquent taxes and assessments of $216,000. The sales yielded almost
$74,000 in delinquent taxes, so over $142,000 had to be abated. In addition, over $1500 in quantifiable administrative costs were not recovered,
and the very high nonquantifiable administrative costs were not recap-

Table 2–8
Quantifiable Administrative Costs for Cleveland Parcels Sold at Sheriff's Sales, 1969–1974

	1969	1970	1971	1973	1974
Total Cleveland parcels sold	14	34	20	14	31
Total cost	$4631	$13,620	$8742	$6067	$12,074
Average cost per parcel	$331	$400	$437	$433	$389
Sheriff's fees—average	$42	$28	$29	$28	$37
range	$17–$106	$15–$115	$17–$100	$16–$57	$23–$209
Appraiser's fees—average	$41	$46	$50	$45	$39
range	$30–$52	$45–$51	$45–$90	$45	$45–$90
Advertising fees—average	$52	$65	$35	$91	$85
range	$44–$99	$43–$108	$72–$123	$72–$132	$75–$269
Actual clerk's cost[a]—average	$190	$257	$268	$264	$221
range	$117–$324	$125–$513	$103–$458	$155–$413	$146–$405
Sheriff's deed fee—average	$5	$5	$5	$5	$8
range	$5	$5	$5	$5	$5–$10

Source: Cuyahoga County Sheriff's Distribution of Sale Packets.

[a]Clerk of Courts costs include payments for clerk, sheriff, legal news, legal news publication, referee, recorder, title search, other county sheriffs, clerk on order of sale, legal news abstract, sheriff on order of sale, title examiner, commissioners, mileage, and certification.

tured at all. (In fact, there is no way within the existing system to recapture the county's general administrative costs for processing delinquent parcels—even if the tax sales produce enough revenues to cover such costs.) As shown in Table 2–9, another $15,000 were spent on administrative costs for parcels that did not sell.

Almost $45,000 in delinquent taxes were recovered in the 1973 and 1974 sheriff's sales, but over $111,000 in delinquent taxes and quantifiable administrative costs were written off on properties that sold. Most of the loss was in abated taxes. Because only 23 percent of the offered parcels were actually sold, however, considerable administrative costs were incurred for properties that did not sell. Further attempts to sell those parcels, at either sheriff's or auditor's sales, would add administrative costs that would be less and less likely to be recaptured.

Predictably, only a small proportion of the total delinquent taxes due were recovered through the 1969 and 1972 forfeiture sales in Cuyahoga County. As indicated in Table 2–10, over 60 percent of the 437 parcels sold had sales prices that represented no more than 30 percent of the taxes due on them. Slightly over $72,000 in delinquent taxes were recovered in the two sales, but over $300,000 were abated. Figures were not available on the administrative costs incurred in bringing the parcels to the point of forfeiture sales.

Table 2–9
Recovery of Delinquent Taxes and Administrative Costs on Cleveland Parcels Offered at Sheriff's Sales, 1969–1971

Year of Sale	Number of Parcels That Sold	Net Losses on Parcels That Sold (Taxes & Administrative Costs)	Number of Parcels That Did Not Sell	Delinquent Taxes on Parcels That Did Not Sell	Partial Administrative Costs for Parcels That Did Not Sell[a]
1969	14	$ 7,271	42	$147,269	$ 4,619
1970	34	$101,529	49	$159,675	$ 6,010
1971	20	$ 35,281	30	$ 72,958	$ 4,562
Total	68	$144,081	121	$379,902	$15,191

Source: Cuyahoga County Sheriff's List of Properties Offered at Foreclosure Sales; Cuyahoga County Sheriff's Distribution of Sale Packets; Cuyahoga County Auditor's Duplicate of Real and Public Utility Property.

[a]This figure does not include the clerk's costs, which usually amount to over 60 percent of the quantifiable costs (see Table 2–8). Administrative costs for the parcels that did not sell probably totaled almost $40,000.

Table 2–10

Forfeiture Sale Prices as a Percent of Delinquent Taxes Due, 1969 and 1972

Sales Prices as a % of Delinquent Taxes Due	% of Parcels Sold in 1969	% of Parcels Sold in 1972
1–5%	9.2%	10.8
6–10%	14.4	19.8
11–20%	15.4	26.5
21–30%	11.3	16.5
31–40%	10.2	7.0
41–50%	7.2	6.6
51–100%	16.4	10.3
Over 100%	10.8	2.5
No information	5.1	—
	100.0%	100.0%
Number of parcels sold	195	242

Source: Cuyahoga County Auditor's Tax Duplicate of Real and Public Utility Property and Forfeited Land List.

Note: These figures reflect only the public liens against sale properties. No account is taken of the administrative costs of bringing the properties to sale.

Tax Status of Foreclosed Delinquent Parcels After Sale

The primary goal of the tax-foreclosure process is to return delinquent properties to the tax duplicate. Failure to recover the full amount of outstanding delinquencies at tax sales can perhaps be justified if the sold parcels again begin producing tax revenue. This can happen only if the properties have considerable intrinsic value, which usually means that their delinquency was a result of the former owners' personal financial difficulties or mismanagement. Delinquency in many of Cleveland's neighborhoods is a result not only of individuals' financial problems, but also of forces that have negatively affected real estate values.

Population has declined in these areas, as have the relative income levels of remaining residents. Rents have failed to keep pace with increasing costs, so maintenance has been deferred and housing has become substandard. The deteriorated physical environment, fear for personal safety, and lack of confidence in the city school system make these areas unacceptable to middle-income families, which can afford to choose among a wide variety of city and suburban residential locations. Those who remain in the areas cannot support the operation of even the existing, poorly maintained structures. Extensive rehabilitation or new construction is usually out of the question without substantial governmental involvement and subsidy.

The relatively low purchase prices of Cleveland properties at tax sales reflect the new owners' perceptions of the parcels' values. Purchasers of foreclosed or forfeited real estate appear reluctant to invest any additional funds in their newly acquired properties. Parcels are becoming delinquent again within a few years after purchase at tax sales. Almost one-half of the parcels sold at the 1969, 1970, and 1971 sheriff's sales were delinquent again by 1973. Over 40 percent of the parcels sold at sheriff's sales in 1973 and 1974 already had outstanding delinquent taxes listed on the 1974 tax duplicate.[e] Almost 60 percent of the parcels sold at the forfeiture sales in 1969 and 1972 were delinquent again by 1974.[4]

The acceptance of low bids at tax sales stimulates speculation in delinquent property. Nearly 60 percent of the parcels sold at the 1969 and 1972 forfeiture sales were purchased by one of ten individuals or groups, and approximately 57 percent of these properties became delinquent again. About 30 percent of the properties sold at the forfeiture sales were acquired by four persons who apparently worked together. Two of those individuals also purchased property at the sheriff's sales, though the higher prices at sheriff's sales generally seem to have discouraged speculation. Speculation patterns were not discernible at the sheriff's sales in 1969, 1970, and 1971.

Tax sale purchasers may hope that the city will acquire their new parcels for renewal activities, or that the properties will regain their former values someday. With the minimal investment required at tax sales, they have little to lose; however, the general public has substantial investment in these parcels, including unpaid taxes, maintenance expenditures for demolition of abandoned structures and for vacant lot cleanup, and unrecovered administrative costs for foreclosure processing. It would be more appropriate if any future increases in the values of delinquent properties were to accrue to the public as compensation for lost revenues. The maintenance costs are already covered by the city in many cases, so the additional holding costs would not be high. In addition, if the public were to obtain title to delinquent parcels that could not be sold for a reasonable proportion of the outstanding taxes and liens, it would facilitate future redevelopment of the inner-city areas where these properties tend to be concentrated.

Although redevelopment will not be feasible for many years in most of these areas, it seems unwise for the public to lose control of foreclosed parcels at prices that are often inadequate to cover administrative costs. Little is accomplished when the ownership of such parcels is turned over to individuals who lack interest in meeting the basic obligations of prop-

---

[e]The tax duplicate for a given year is published in December of that year. Thus the 1974 tax duplicate appears in December 1974.

erty ownership. If these parcels become delinquent again shortly after they are purchased at tax sales—and about half of them do—the costly administrative procedure is just repeated. This can happen over and over again, with the taxpayers losing each time.

Conclusions

The foreclosure process in Cuyahoga County takes three to four times as long as the minimum period anticipated by the Ohio tax sale statute. Within the first three years of delinquency, which is close to the minimum time in which foreclosure could technically be completed, about one-half of the properties are redeemed by their owners. These owners were probably faced with only temporary financial difficulties, but in any event, they were clearly interested in retaining control of their properties. They are not contributors to Cleveland's long-term delinquency problem.

The length of time that a property is allowed to remain delinquent prior to loss of title has several important implications:

1. A long period of redemption, whether occasioned by statute or by practice, encourages owners to avoid paying taxes because they are not threatened with immediate loss of their properties. The owner of a marginally profitable property, for example, can collect rents but neglect to pay taxes and thereby extend the property's economic life by a few more years. If continued ownership is considered desirable at the point of actual foreclosure, the taxes and 10-percent penalty can be paid.
2. After a property has been delinquent for a number of years, the amount of unpaid taxes often exceeds the parcel's value. If owners of such properties were threatened with foreclosure earlier, when the total outstanding delinquencies were lower and the properties still had value, the redemption rate might be considerably higher.
3. In deteriorated areas, many tax-delinquent properties have been abandoned by their owners. Buildings are often vandalized and seriously damaged after abandonment. Thus by the time many parcels are offered at tax sales, the structures—if they are still standing—are worth very little.

The existing tax-foreclosure/sale procedure as it operates in Cuyahoga County is costly, particularly with respect to the less marketable properties in Cleveland's inner city. Modifications in some of the practices listed below could result in substantial savings:

1. Repeated advertisements (twice in two newspapers) of tax delinquent parcels after certification and before each sheriff's and auditor's sale.
2. Elaborate notification procedures, during which both the auditor's and the prosecutor's offices attempt to locate all the individuals with interests in tax delinquent properties and notify them of foreclosure proceedings. (Although the Ohio statute provides that "any number of lots and lands" may be joined in one action, the Cuyahoga County Prosecutor follows this process only when a number of delinquent parcels have a common owner.)
3. Equal treatment of all properties, including valuable and readily marketable properties as well as parcels with low assessed values, vacant lots in deteriorated areas, and slivers of land or other remnant parcels created by public acquisition for freeways and other uses.
4. Routine appraisal of delinquent parcels, which means that each property is appraised by three persons at a cost of $15 per appraiser. After being appraised, properties cannot be sold at sheriff's sales for less than two-thirds of the average appraised value.
5. The need to hold a succession of foreclosure and forfeiture sales, at which many properties are offered at prices well above their marketable values.
6. For individual properties that sell at prices in excess of the debt owed and the expenses involved in the sale, return of the overages to the original owners. Because of this provision, the taxing jurisdiction does not have an opportunity to capture sale benefits, though it suffers many losses on properties that sell for less than their outstanding liens.

These and other administrative points regarding the current foreclosure process in Cuyahoga County are discussed further in Chapter 7, where the recommendations from this study are presented.

A tax-foreclosure procedure that requires eventual sale of delinquent parcels has the following results in the weak real estate markets now existing in many areas of Cleveland and other central cities:

1. Lack of demand will necessitate offering individual parcels at more than one sale before they can be disposed of. (Potential investors in Cleveland wait until a forfeiture sale, where prices are at their lowest, to purchase delinquent land.)
2. Parcels will be sold at low prices, often far less than the administrative costs of bringing them to sale.
3. Only a fraction of the delinquent taxes and special assessments will actually be recovered; the remainder will have to be abated.

4. Parcels will often become delinquent again shortly after they are purchased at tax sales. The new owners, who have invested a minimal amount in purchasing these properties, are not anxious to spend much more in maintaining their investments.
5. Property sales at "bargain basement" prices invite speculation.
6. After purchased parcels become delinquent again, the costly administrative procedure must be repeated, and perhaps repeated again.

A substantial proportion of delinquent tax revenues are never recovered under the existing procedures. Although relatively minor changes in the statutory administrative procedures would reduce current losses, a system requiring the sale of unmarketable tax delinquent properties is doomed to failure. The elimination of multiple offerings of individual parcels would save on administrative costs, and a reduction of the time that parcels could remain delinquent before foreclosure would encourage many owners to pay their taxes longer. However, neither of these possible actions addresses the basic real estate market problem.

Under the current foreclosure process, the public receives little or no compensation for lost revenues. Delinquent parcels are frequently sold at prices lower than the administrative costs of bringing them to sale. (Fortunately, only a small proportion of the eligible parcels are actually offered at tax sales.) If the foreclosure procedure were altered so that the public would obtain title to tax delinquent lands, any subsequent appreciation in property values would accrue to the public and would offer partial compensation for lost revenues. Public control over the parcels would also facilitate eventual redevelopment of deteriorated inner-city areas.

Given Cleveland's experience with the existing foreclosure procedure, it is apparent that the assumptions underlying that procedure no longer represent the real estate market realities in many areas of the city. The foreclosure procedure results neither in recovery of delinquent tax revenues nor in productive return of delinquent properties to the tax duplicate. Changes in the process are necessary to reflect economic and financial realities and to insure that the public receives compensation for lost tax revenues.

Notes

1. See "Revenue and Taxation—Collection of Delinquent Real Estate Taxes: Legislating Protection of the Delinquent Property Owner in an Era of Super-Marketable Tax Titles," *De Paul Law Review* 19 (1969) 360–365.

2. The description of the statutory process is adapted from the *Ohio Revised Code*, Chapters 5721 and 5723.

3. This statement is based on examination of the results of the 1969–1971 and 1973–1974 sheriff's sales and the 1969 and 1972 auditor's forfeiture sales.

4. These conclusions are based on an analysis of the Cuyahoga County Auditor's Forfeited Land List and the Sheriff's Lists of Property Offered at Foreclosure Sales.

3

A Model for Change:
St. Louis's Land
Reutilization Authority

Ohio's foreclosure process and its increasingly apparent inadequacies for handling the number and type of delinquent properties in the city of Cleveland are typical of the tax collection systems operating in states and urban areas across the country. The need for new procedures has been recognized as taxing officials have come to realize that rising tax delinquency is usually a symptom of weakening inner-city real estate markets. Increasing proportions of the delinquent parcels in central cities that are brought to foreclosure sale do not have sufficient intrinsic value to cover back taxes and administrative costs. Property-owners also seem to be resorting to nonpayment of taxes as a short-term method of improving their cash flows, thereby postponing abandonment. The recognition of this latter trend has led to the hypothesis that delinquent properties, which are often poorly maintained, have a blighting influence on their immediate neighborhoods. Rapid foreclosure has been seen as a method of fixing or removing these "bad teeth" from otherwise reasonably sound residential areas.

A number of taxing jurisdictions have responded to increasing central-city tax delinquency by revising their foreclosure procedures. The most common approach has been to accelerate foreclosure—either by improving administrative processing to meet the minimum legal time limits or by changing the state enabling legislation to shorten those time limits. In Newark, for example, the city tax collector began to enforce the tax collection foreclosure law strictly, particularly for vacant land and buildings. Then the Newark Real Estate Commission adopted and widely publicized a bimonthly auction procedure to dispose of foreclosed properties. Within one-and-a-half years from the inception of the program, auctions led to the disposition of over 400 parcels and the generation of about $1 million in sales revenues (twice the proceeds obtained in sheriff's sales in the previous ten years). The success of the Newark program prompted the New Jersey State Legislature to pass legislation enabling all cities in the state to take title quickly to vacant properties.

Newark's program aims at returning delinquent properties to the tax rolls. By turning over a large number of properties, the presumption is that there will be net gains even if a relatively high percentage soon become delinquent again. Pressing need for revenues seems to have outweighed concern for increased administrative expense and what might be called consumer protection. To reduce speculation and to encourage

53

owner-occupancy, a homesteading provision was added to the auction procedure for residential properties of under six units. Initial asking prices are lowered for buyers who agree to bring buildings up to code standards within one year and reside in them for five years. Tax abatement is not offered to homesteaders, nor are homesteaders counseled about the probable costs of rehabilitation or the likely market values of their improved properties. Although the homesteaded buildings are in diverse neighborhoods, publicity about the availability of this sort of "bargain" is open to charges of public exploitation of persons uninformed about trends in inner-city real estate markets.

Programs aimed primarily at rapidly returning delinquent properties to tax-paying status are both the simplest and the most common response to increased tax delinquency. However, they do not address the complexity of the problem, nor are they likely to be cost-effective in the long run because increasing proportions of the formerly delinquent parcels can be expected to recycle through the foreclosure process. When administrative costs exceed the sale prices of the parcels, this system becomes counterproductive. The public also loses control over parcels in which it has a substantial investment, and for which it may have to pay later if the properties are part of a renewal effort.

St. Louis has the most comprehensive foreclosure system that was designed to address many of the complex issues involved in the central-city tax delinquency problem. Missouri's Land Reutilization Law, which was passed in 1971,[1] enabled St. Louis to (1) foreclose on tax delinquent properties within two years; (2) reduce processing costs by filing one suit against a large number of parcels; and (3) establish a Land Reutilization Authority that could purchase, manage, hold, sell, or lease foreclosed properties that could not be sold for at least the back taxes.

Precedence for individual components of the Missouri legislation exists in the more traditional tax collection and foreclosure statutes of other states. For instance, eight western states have a foreclosure procedure in which, after a five-year redemption period, delinquent properties are automatically sold to the state instead of to private purchasers. Other states, such as South Dakota, Minnesota, and Maryland, give local taxing bodies power to reasonably limit the costly advertising and owner-notification components of foreclosure. In Maryland, for example, owners need not be notified by mail; instead, announcements of foreclosure proceedings can be advertised in one general-circulation newspaper. Also, Maryland cities can purchase lands not sold at foreclosure sales for the amount of taxes and costs (such as interest penalties, administrative costs, legal fees, advertising expenses). However, a Maryland foreclosure sale is just a preliminary act, after which there is a relatively long redemption period. In addition, the purchaser bears the burden of obtaining clear title to a foreclosed parcel.

Some states allow collection agencies to engage private attorneys when the volume of cases is beyond the capacity of the government's legal staff. In a number of states, consolidated suits can be brought against many delinquent parcels, avoiding the costs incurred when individual suits are filed against each parcel. Although two or more tax sales are often required before a government agency or a private purchaser can obtain clear and marketable title to a foreclosed property, some states require only one sale, which somewhat reduces the time necessary to perfect title.

In some states, several of these streamlining procedures are available to local taxing jurisdictions. However, these combinations of expanded legal powers and efficient administrative practices have not accelerated the foreclosure process in other cities as much as in St. Louis. Largely because of its emphasis on three key factors—rapid foreclosure, reduced administrative costs, and local government acquisition of low value properties—the St. Louis Land Reutilization Authority (LRA) has attracted a great deal of attention from other jurisdictions.

When our study began in Cleveland, we anticipated recommending that similar legislation be introduced in the state legislature to enable the creation of an LRA in Cleveland and other large Ohio cities. However, our research findings led us to the conclusion that the Missouri legislation contains pitfalls that could result in costly new responsibilities for city governments. Therefore we finally recommended that a significantly modified version of the St. Louis model be developed in Cleveland. To assist readers in following the reasoning behind our recommendations (which are set forth in Chapter 7), we will summarize the procedures and operations of the St. Louis LRA before we present our field survey results and analyses.

Structure of the St. Louis LRA

Missouri passed legislation establishing the City of St. Louis Land Reutilization Authority in 1971. At that time the city collected only 90 percent of the property taxes due, a decrease from 99 percent in 1950. About 9 percent of the properties in the city were tax delinquent, and a sheriff's sale had not been held for twenty years. Faced with declining property tax collection efficiency, a special task force analyzed foreclosure procedures used by other Missouri cities, especially Kansas City (in Jackson County). Then a law was designed exclusively for the city of St. Louis, though it was patterned after the Jackson County Land Trust.

The state legislation introduced by St. Louis representatives accelerated foreclosure in an attempt to increase tax payment by threatening delinquent owners with more immediate loss of their properties. It also enabled the creation of the Land Reutilization Authority. The LRA's purpose is to return non-revenue-producing land to the tax rolls or to place it under public control to improve residential, industrial, and employment opportunities in the city. To accomplish this goal, the LRA is empowered to manage, or to sell, transfer, or otherwise dispose of delinquent parcels. It can also accept grants of any interest in vacant real property. (This provision would have to be exercised with care—say, in a situation where the city would be joint owner of an illegally occupied building if one partner gave his or her share to the LRA to compensate for delinquent taxes.)

As we discuss later in the chapter, the Land Reutilization Authority differs in many ways from the Kansas City/Jackson County Land Trust on which it was partially modeled. One major difference is the program's administration. The LRA was designed to operate in St. Louis's unique city-county governmental structure. Unlike all other cities in Missouri, St. Louis became independent of its county in 1876. As a result, the city government assumed county functions, including the power of property tax collection. This unusual combination of traditional city and county governmental powers does not exist in Kansas City and Cleveland, which have countywide collection systems.

The LRA is administered by a salaried program director and three commissioners who serve without compensation. The commissioners are appointed by the comptroller, the mayor, and the board of education. In addition to the LRA staff—which usually consists of the program director and a staff of four to eight people who process foreclosure suits—persons in the collector's office, the circuit clerk's office and the sheriff's office also assist with foreclosure proceedings. A 2-percent fee is paid to the collector for collection services, and the sheriff also receives a fee for parcels that are sold.

Administrative costs for the LRA are about $30 per parcel per year. This figure does not include the legal counsel provided free by the city, or the donation of office space in city hall to house the LRA. These contributions of office space and legal staff reduce the LRA's operating costs. Initially, the city loaned $20,000 to the LRA, which has since been repaid. The city provides an annual appropriation for LRA staff salaries, but this has also been returned at the end of each year. The LRA receives revenues from the sale and management of properties, and the agency had a budget surplus of $200,000 in early 1975. The LRA is very proud of being self-supporting, and its commitment to continued solvency is reflected in the agency's current operating procedures.

The St. Louis Tax-Foreclosure Process

Missouri's Land Reutilization Law reduces the time and cost of foreclosing against tax delinquent properties by streamlining the administrative process. Prior to legislative changes, the procedure for acquiring delinquent properties took a minimum of three years, though the normal processing time was much longer. One of the major changes instituted in 1971 permits the collector of revenue to file one suit against a large number of properties that have been delinquent for two years. Previously, consolidated suits could be brought against a large number of properties only if each property had been delinquent for more than four years. After the creation of the LRA, other streamlining administrative procedures permitted by the old and new laws were followed more strictly (for example, bringing suit against properties instead of owners, reducing the advertising and mailing efforts required to notify owners of foreclosure, and decreasing the number of full-time attorneys required to process large numbers of delinquent parcels).

The first step in the foreclosure process is the collection of data on parcels delinquent for more than two years that are to be included in a land tax suit. Although any number of parcels may be included, the collector of revenue usually joins 500 parcels in each suit for efficient processing. This procedure alone substantially reduces the time and cost involved in foreclosing against properties. Reportedly, about 500 parcels can be sued at one time for the same cost as individual suits against 25 properties.

To avoid possible criticism for arbitrarily choosing parcels to be included in a suit, the collector's office developed a method for selecting the delinquent parcels to be joined together. Initially, the collector included only properties delinquent since before 1968, using a computerized system that selected every delinquent property on each consecutive city block until 500 parcels were chosen. After all the parcels that had become delinquent prior to 1968 were redeemed or sued, the same selection process was used for parcels that had been delinquent for just two to four years. The delinquent buildings were often severely deteriorated by the time foreclosure action was initiated against them, and many were vacant lots or contained unoccupied buildings. By early 1976 no parcels that had become delinquent after 1971 had been included in the St. Louis collector's land tax suits. Therefore because the city had not yet foreclosed on large numbers of parcels containing occupied buildings, the Land Reutilization Authority had not been required to manage many occupied structures.

Having selected approximately 500 parcels to be sued, the St. Louis collector of revenue proceeds to the second step of the foreclosure process—petitioning for suit of the parcels. The petition has the same effect on every parcel as a corporate suit instituted to foreclose the tax lien(s) against any individual parcel. The key element of the joined suits against numerous delinquent parcels is that the property and not the owner is brought under suit. Thus "due process" of foreclosure is achieved by *in rem* proceedings (against the parcel) versus *in personem* proceedings (against the owner). In Cleveland a hybrid method is used, whereby the foreclosure action is deemed an *in rem* action, but the unwieldy *in personem* procedure is followed to execute foreclosure. Thus an expensive title search is used, and every interested person or entity is made party to the suit, located, and provided with specific notice. The costs in money and time are substantial.

This *in rem* procedure reduces the time and cost spent in notifying property owners of foreclosure proceedings because it deems notice by publication adequate if the owner cannot be reached at his or her last known address. The *in rem* proceeding subjects the land to payment of the tax. No personal judgment is rendered against the owner because the tax is recovered from the land itself. It is not necessary to name as defendants all parties with an interest, immediate or remote, in the property. The constitutionality of the Land Tax Collection Law was challenged, but the Missouri Supreme Court ruled in effect that once taxes on land are assessed in accordance with due process, the owners or lien holders may be presumed to know that the land will be sold for nonpayment of taxes.[2]

In the third step of the foreclosure process, the collector places a foreclosure notice in a daily newspaper of general circulation. The notice appears for four successive weeks on the same day of each week. A newspaper of general circulation rather than a legal newspaper of records was purposely required by the Municipal Land Reutilization Law in order to have evidence that a good-faith effort was made to notify the owners. In addition, the collector mails a personal notification of the foreclosure proceedings to the last address of record. Copies of all notifications are filed with the circuit clerk as evidence that the collector of revenues' office has fulfilled its obligations and so that the notifications can be used when the suit is taken to court.

To further reduce the administrative cost of tax foreclosure and to expedite the process, the collector employs private attorneys on an "as needed" basis instead of maintaining a large in-house legal staff. Missouri state legislation allows a maximum attorney's fee equal to 6 percent of the amount of taxes actually collected, plus $2 per parcel for each suit filed and unpublished. A slightly higher additional fee of $5 is permitted for each suit that is filed and published.

Property-owners are allowed sixty days following the first newspaper publication of foreclosure to redeem their properties. An owner can either pay the total amount of taxes and accrued costs or enter into an installment contract to make monthly or bimonthly payments over a period that generally cannot exceed two years. If the owner does not redeem the property within sixty days, the court can render judgment to foreclose upon the parcel. Unredeemed parcels of at least six months' standing are included in the sheriff's foreclosure sale, the date of which is advertised in a daily newspaper and fixed for twenty-one days following the notice. Prior to the sale, owners have another opportunity to redeem their properties. For those who pay taxes and costs in installments, a strict payment schedule is observed. If one installment payment is missed, the parcel is slated for the next sheriff's foreclosure sale.

The final step in the foreclosure process is the sheriff's sale, which is conducted for three days. If there is no bid during that time equal to the full amount of the tax bills, penalties, attorney's fees and administrative costs, the Land Reutilization Authority bids the full amount and obtains the title to the property. However, the LRA does not reimburse the taxing bodies until it sells the property. The sheriff's sale provides a marketable title to each parcel, conveying the whole interest of every person having or claiming any right, interest, or lien on a property. When the LRA purchases a parcel, it holds the title in trust for the local taxing authorities with interests in the real estate.

The proceeds of sales to buyers other than the LRA are used to pay the costs of newspaper advertisements and personal notices, appraisers' and attorneys' fees, and taxes (including principal, interest, and penalties) in that order of priority. If any funds remain, they are returned to the previous property owner or are forfeited to the state if no one claims them within two years. Advertising expenses and appraisers' and attorneys' fees for properties that are not sold at the foreclosure sale are paid from current tax collections by the collector of revenue and then are reimbursed by the LRA when the properties are sold.

The LRA's Property Management Capabilities

The St. Louis Land Reutilization Authority assumes possession of all properties for which no acceptable bids are received at the foreclosure sale. After acquisition, the LRA inventories and appraises the parcels and classifies them as (1) suitable for private use, (2) suitable for public use, or (3) suitable for landbanking. The LRA has the power to manage, maintain, rent, lease, insure, and alter real estate that it is holding. It may also receive gifts of whole or partial real estate interests in unoccupied buildings. The LRA commissioners must approve specific actions concerning properties being held by the LRA.

The LRA is to sell property suitable for private use for a price that is at least two-thirds of the appraised value. Property for public reuse may be transferred at no cost except administrative expenses if the commissioners vote unanimously in support of the public reuse. If land is transferred to another public agency at no cost and if that agency sells the parcel within ten years, the proceeds are turned over to the LRA for distribution to the appropriate taxing authorities.

As of January 1976, the LRA was reportedly receiving rents from at least fifty residential buildings that were occupied at the time of public acquisition. Rents were collected on these and other nonresidential properties (namely, two parking lots and one business) by a private realty firm that received 5 percent of the rental income as its management fee. The LRA has tried to provide safe living conditions in its legally occupied buildings, although the buildings do not necessarily conform to housing codes. To limit its management role, the Land Reutilization Authority does not accept new tenants when its former tenants leave. There are no formal mechanisms to assist in tenant relocation, and the LRA process is not subject to the provisions of the Uniform Relocation Act of 1970, which requires that relocation assistance be given to persons displaced by government actions.

When the LRA was established, its planners had not anticipated the receipt of occupied residential buildings at the end of the foreclosure process. As it has turned out, however, the LRA has received both legally and illegally occupied housing units. Illegal occupancy occurs when squatters settle in previously vacant buildings. Squatters occupied an estimated 10 percent of the housing units that the LRA acquired in 1975, and illegal occupancy has been a continuing problem in St. Louis.

The LRA's Operating Experience

Between January 1972 and Spring 1975, the collector's, circuit clerk's, and sheriff's offices in St. Louis processed 21 law suits against 8757 tax delinquent parcels. Of this total, 1581 parcels had been fully redeemed by their owners; 1120 were being redeemed on two-year installment contracts; and 4869 had been forfeited to the LRA. Approximately 20 percent of the forfeited parcels had structural improvements, many of which were vacant and abandoned. In the first two foreclosure filings, approximately 50 properties were included in each suit to discover unforeseen complications. As no problems arose, approximately 4 to 6 suits, each including 500 parcels, were then processed annually.

After the accelerated foreclosure process was instituted, property tax collection increased from 90 to 96 percent of taxes due; LRA staff anticipate even greater improvement. Relatively few parcels had been sold to private purchasers by 1975. In 1973, 22 parcels were sold by the LRA, and the prices after costs were deducted covered only about 45 percent of the properties' delinquent taxes. The LRA sold about 138 parcels in 1974, at prices that totaled about 99.6 percent of the delinquent taxes. Another 230 parcels were sold in 1975. In addition to these transactions, several hundred housing units are leased to homesteaders who are renovating the buildings, and some vacant and improved properties are rented by the private realty company that is under contract to the LRA. Land speculation by private buyers purchasing LRA properties has largely been avoided, both because the LRA has used discretion in approving sales and because most LRA-owned properties have limited immediate market potential.

It is apparently unusual for properties sold at sheriff's sales or by the LRA to become tax delinquent again. For those properties being redeemed on a two-year installment plan, missed payments are also infrequent. The statute allows the property to be placed on the next notice of a sheriff's sale if an installment payment is missed, thereby avoiding the necessity of repeating the total foreclosure process. Approximately ten properties have missed a payment at the time of each sheriff's sale notice, and these properties have usually been redeemed prior to the sale.

The LRA has not yet adopted a long-term disposition or management strategy for its parcels, though informal coordination has been established with other public agencies.[3] In early 1976 its primary uses of land were as follows:

1. Holding land for the Urban Renewal Agency and the Planned Industrial Expansion Authority for development of an industrial park. For example, the LRA accumulated forty-three vacant parcels constituting five acres, and then sold them to the Planned Industrial Expansion Authority for $1000. This represents about one-third of the area of a proposed industrial park.
2. Holding approximately 40 percent of the land in the area designated by the Community Development Agency for a new town-in-town.
3. Homesteading properties in neighborhoods deemed viable by the LRA director.

Most of the improved residential properties disposed of by the LRA are sold as part of its homesteading program. Potential buyers are required to lease their units with an option to purchase until they are brought up to housing code standards. The lease period cannot exceed two years, and title is not transferred until the unit is fully restored. The purchase price is based on the market value of the unit in its original, unrehabilitated condition, but the price cannot be less than two-thirds of the appraised value or less than $100. The minimum down-payment is 10 percent, although 25 percent is preferred. After an analysis of applicants' personal assets, the LRA selects those households that have a discretionary fund of at least $50 to $100 per month. Of those who apply for homesteading, approximately 15 percent are turned down.

To qualify for homesteading, a family must: (1) be financially able to restore, repair, and rehabilitate their building to meet standards set forth in the lease they sign and to maintain the property once it has been restored (the LRA estimates that repair costs range from $5000 to $10,000 for each property); (2) agree to improve the property by removing derelict parts, exterior renovation, landscaping, sidewalk repairs, and restoration of the interior to meet housing code requirements; (3) be a normal family unit of one man and one woman; and (4) be of good moral character.[4]

These requirements are somewhat flexible, and LRA negotiates each homesteading contract on an individual basis, with an eye to the particular needs of both the property and its buyer. The typical homesteading couple in St. Louis has a combined income of $16,000.

The LRA's primary concern in its homesteading program is to return properties to the tax rolls. By requiring more than a token purchase price and by insisting that homesteaders bring their buildings up to code standards without financial help, the city's goal has been to attract stable families who will not abandon their units later. By spring 1975 more than 300 abandoned structures had been homesteaded since the program's inception in early 1974. The LRA planned to place 200 more buildings on the market by the end of 1976. Many of the units are located in historically significant neighborhoods or in areas of limited abandonment, and spot checks indicated that units were being brought up to code. Very few units have reverted to LRA, and those units were returned primarily because of homesteaders' personal problems, such as having to move out of town, or becoming divorced. To avoid residential real estate speculation, structures with more than four units are not sold by the LRA for homesteading.

The Jackson County/Kansas City Foreclosure Process

The 1971 St. Louis Municipal Land Reutilization Law, as mentioned earlier, was based on the Jackson County Land Tax Collection Law, which was enacted in 1943 and still pertains in Jackson County and so applies to most of Kansas City, Missouri. Several changes were made in the new 1971 law, however, to accommodate St. Louis's unique city-county governmental structure and to improve on some aspects of the Jackson County law.

One major difference between the Jackson County law and the St. Louis law is the time permitted between delinquency and foreclosure and the number of years of delinquent taxes that can be collected. In St. Louis action can begin after a minimum of two years of tax delinquency, whereas in Jackson County the collector can initiate foreclosure only after a property's city and/or county real estate taxes have been delinquent for four years. Furthermore, if action is not brought against a Jackson County parcel during the fifth year of delinquency, the county forfeits its right to collect taxes that are more than four years delinquent. Action taken against a parcel in January 1976, for example, could not include unpaid taxes assessed for January 1970. Unpaid taxes for January 1971 and for the subsequent years could have been included in a foreclosure action in January 1976.

Jackson County's owner notification procedure also differs from St. Louis's. Whereas St. Louis advertises in newspapers of general circulation, Jackson County attempts personal notification through several mailings, even though the foreclosure process is an *in rem* action as in St. Louis.

Another major difference between the two foreclosure laws is the methods that property owners can use to redeem their parcels. In Jackson County, despite a centralized countywide collection procedure, individual municipalities can dictate specific practices to be followed. Both St. Louis and Jackson County permit owners to pay delinquent taxes in installments, but this is not allowed within the boundaries of Kansas City. Jackson County's provision for installment payments is stricter than St. Louis's; the county requires a down-payment of at least one-third of the total amount due.

The Jackson County Land Trust, created in 1945, is empowered to manage, sell, and dispose of tax delinquent parcels. Like the St. Louis Land Reutilization Authority, the Land Trust has three commissioners; however, they are selected by the county court, the city council of Kansas City, and the board of directors of the school district with the largest population in the county. The appointing authorities in St. Louis are the mayor, the comptroller, and the board of directors of the school board. The St. Louis commissioners are not paid, whereas those in Jackson County receive an annual salary of $2400. A salaried director administers the Land Trust with a staff of one chief field deputy, one chief accountant, four assistant field deputies, stenographers, clerical employees, and attorneys.

After thirty-one years of operation and an original backlog of some 15,000 properties, the Land Trust now holds only about 1200 parcels. The director estimates that about 10 of these parcels have legally occupied improvements, although a much larger number are occupied by squatters, especially in Kansas City. The percentage of improved parcels forfeited to the trust is increasing, but the agency has no existing management or tenant relocation capacity. The Land Trust is empowered to manage properties that it holds; however, rent is not even collected on its small number of legally occupied structures. The director of the Land Trust estimates that approximately 100 parcels are sold each year, most of which are unimproved. The trust has no formal property disposition or landbanking strategy.

Conclusions

Of the numerous foreclosure procedures in operation across the country, only the Missouri processes combine both legislation and administrative practices that enable rapid foreclosure and acquisition by a special public agency of properties that cannot be sold for prices high enough to cover back taxes. Although this model is fast and efficient, a city contemplating a change in its foreclosure process must ask whether the Missouri method best serves the public interest. The St. Louis LRA's experience suggests that state legislation enabling rapid foreclosure on all types of properties may have adverse effects on the strength and viability of inner-city neighborhoods and on the governmental agencies serving them.

Many factors should be considered before the St. Louis model is replicated. Key among these are the following

1. The threat of foreclosure within two years of initial tax delinquency appears to improve tax collections. In light of our analysis of low-income housing markets (Chapter 6), however, this procedure may also accelerate abandonment and/or city acquisition of occupied residential structures that are no longer economically feasible investments.
2. The acquisition of occupied buildings poses serious management problems for a city agency. The tenants usually will not be able to afford rents that are high enough to cover operating and maintenance costs, or the properties would have been sold for market prices at foreclosure sales. Thus the city has the choice of: (a) managing substandard buildings; (b) subsidizing the operations of the buildings to bring them up to code standards; or (c) relocating the tenants and demolishing the buildings. The LRA in St. Louis manages the units until the tenants move, then it boards up or demolishes the buildings. A private realty company handles day-to-day management on contract, but the LRA holds title to the properties. It appears that the probability of acquiring more such buildings has caused a slowdown in the processing of foreclosures in St. Louis. As of early 1976,

properties that had become delinquent after 1971 were not yet being foreclosed.

3. It is in the long-term public interest for an agency such as the LRA to acquire properties with very low or negligible market values. Properties that are sold at low prices to get them back on the tax rolls have a high probability of becoming delinquent again, necessitating repetition of the costly administrative process. If the properties are held by the city, they can be aggregated for eventual disposition to public or private users. An agency holding such parcels should not be expected to generate revenues in the short run, however; it may not even cover its own administrative costs. Most of these properties will have to be landbanked for some time before they will appreciate in value. The authority might be able to lease a few parcels for parking, storage, and so forth, which will provide some operating revenues. However, pressuring the agency to be self-supporting or profit-making is likely to be counterproductive in the long run.

4. The LRA in St. Louis has encouraged homesteading of abandoned units by families able to afford to bring the buildings up to code, which usually means total rehabilitation. This solution is not viable for many properties, though it can work in historic districts or other carefully selected neighborhoods where the buildings have architectural merit, where few low-income residents remain, and where public facilities and services are improved to support the private redevelopment efforts. In most neighborhoods, however, there will be too few homesteaders to have a measurable impact on deteriorated areas, and the market values of their rehabilitated properties often will be far below their investments.

As we will discuss in more detail in later chapters, we believe that an agency like the Land Reutilization Authority is well suited to receive, hold, and eventually dispose of vacant inner-city parcels that have low values. Vacant lots and empty buildings pose minimal management problems for a local government. Occupied buildings, on the other hand, create serious difficulties, and the implications of extensive acquisition or receivership should be evaluated thoroughly before such a program is initiated. Most local governments lack the resources to manage standard housing for low-income tenants, and adverse publicity can be expected to accompany public ownership of substandard housing units.

Notes

1. For a discussion of the development and passage of Missouri's Land Reutilization Law, see Kenneth R. Langsdorf, "Urban Decay,

Property Tax Delinquency: A Solution in St. Louis," *The Urban Lawyer* 5, no. 4 (Fall 1973): 729–747.

2. Spitcaufsky v. Hatten, 182 S.W.2d 86 (Mo. 1944).

3. Analyses aimed toward development of an industrial land disposition strategy for the LRA were prepared by Team Four, Inc. and Lee Carter in April 1975. See *The Reuse of Tax Delinquent Properties,* prepared for the Economic Development Division of the City of St. Louis Community Development Agency.

4. Land Reutilization Authority of the City of St. Louis, "The Saint Louis Plan of Urban Homesteading," January 2, 1974.

4 Classification of Cleveland's Residential Neighborhoods

In Cleveland, as in most other cities, very little was known about the characteristics of tax delinquent properties before our study began. Our initial analysis of the county auditor's records revealed the gross parameters of the delinquency problem. As described in Chapter 1, we found that the incidence of delinquency had increased markedly, especially in the most deteriorated areas of the city. We also learned that the assessed valuations of delinquent parcels were not much lower than those of nondelinquent properties, even though more and more of the former parcels consisted of vacant lots from which the buildings had been removed. Although these findings are important, without knowing what types of properties were delinquent, who owned them, who lived in them, what condition the structures were in, and how many housing units they contained, we could not evaluate the likely impact of introducing a rapid foreclosure process like the one used in St. Louis.

We wanted to generate information that would help answer such questions as:

1. What effects would accelerated foreclosure have on neighborhoods with various proportions of delinquent parcels?
2. What kinds of owners do not pay property taxes (small-scale landlords, large-scale landlords, or owner-occupants)?
3. What are the reasons for tax delinquency among various types of property-owners?
4. If threatened with prompt foreclosure, would the owners of delinquent parcels be willing or able to pay their back taxes?
5. Would rapid foreclosure accelerate the abandonment of properties in the city?
6. What kinds of management problems might the city face if new foreclosure procedures were introduced?

As a means of addressing some of these questions, we decided to inspect over half the improved delinquent parcels in Cleveland, focusing primarily on the physical characteristics of the properties. Our inventory was planned to reveal the types of properties that were delinquent (such as recently cleared land, commercial or industrial buildings, residences), the number of units in residential buildings, the physical condition of the structures, and the extent of occupancy versus abandonment. Thus our

67

goal was to determine the nature of the *supply* of tax delinquent properties, though we also checked on owner occupancy, which is a demand characteristic.

For our overall analysis of *demand*, we relied on four primary sources:

1. Neighborhood characteristics—We gathered general information on the residents of the survey neighborhoods, relying on 1970 Census data and concentrating on such household characteristics as income, age, race, and size.
2. Studies by the City Planning Commission—In previous analyses, Cleveland City Planning Commission staff members examined the low-rent housing market in the city by statistical area (the geographic subdivision that was equated with residential neighborhoods in the current study).[1]
3. Interview data from other cities—The Center for Urban Policy Research at Rutgers University has carried out extensive interview programs with owners of tax delinquent properties in Newark, New York, and Pittsburgh.[2] We drew upon the results of those interviews in evaluating the demand side of the delinquency problem.
4. Survey of large-scale landlords—To assist in analyzing the likely effects of changes in the foreclosure process on the low-rent housing market, Real Estate Research Corporation interviewed large-scale owners of inner-city properties in Cleveland. The findings of that survey are presented in Chapter 6.

The Cleveland City Planning Commission conducted the inventory of tax delinquent properties on a neighborhood-by-neighborhood basis so the findings of the survey could be correlated with small-area housing market analyses. To stratify the sample for extrapolation to citywide totals, we classified all Cleveland's residential neighborhoods according to a five-stage typology used by Real Estate Research Corporation. We classified the thirty-seven residential statistical areas in Cleveland on the basis of a physical inspection and a review of selected socioeconomic characteristics. We did not include two sections of the city, the industrial valley and downtown, in this analysis because of their limited number of housing units. After we classified all the residential areas and analyzed their delinquency rates, we selected representative neighborhoods at various stages of development or decline for the survey.

Five-Stage Classification of Residential Areas

The neighborhood classification system used as the framework for the Cleveland survey evolved through several studies that Real Estate Research Corporation performed for the U. S. Department of Housing and Urban Development.[3] Within the overall process of urban development,[4] RERC identified five major *processes of change* involved in the decline and improvement of neighborhoods. These five processes are normally found to be operating, or to have operated, in neighborhoods that have experienced any significant degree of decline—whether or not that decline was later followed by upgrading. These processes of change are:

1. Physical deterioration
2. Ethnic change
3. Loss of confidence in the neighborhood's future
4. Economic disinvestment
5. Decline in the residents' socioeconomic status.

Correlating changes in these five processes, RERC determined that declining neighborhoods pass through definable stages that are consistent throughout the country. Five general stages have been identified, ranging from healthy neighborhoods to nonviable and heavily abandoned neighborhoods. This typology is quite accurate, though some newer cities do not have neighborhoods in the late stages. To reflect more refined gradations, it is often useful to designate half stages between the more general full stages; this leads to a typology of nine possible stages. Half stages were used in the Cleveland analysis.

The five general stages that RERC has identified in the neighborhood change process are, briefly:

Stage 1 *Healthy neighborhoods:* These are viable neighborhoods that are either relatively new and thriving, or relatively old and stable. No symptoms of decline have yet appeared in them. Some neighborhoods can remain in this stage for many decades if they have highly attractive locations near major amenities.

Stage 2 *Neighborhoods of incipient decline:* These are generally older areas experiencing some functional obsolescence. As older families whose children are grown move out, younger ones with fewer economic resources move in. Minor physical deficiencies in housing units, plus some rising density, begin to appear. The level of public service and the social status of the neighborhood decline somewhat.

Stage 3 *Neighborhoods with decline clearly underway:* Changes begun in Stage 2 become more definite. Renters dominate more and more as tenants, and minor physical deficiencies multiply until visible everywhere. Tenant-landlord relations deteriorate and absentee ownership rises. Conversions to higher density use increase, and overall confidence in the area slackens. Abandonment may begin.

Stage 4 *Neighborhoods accelerating into late stages of decline:* Housing becomes very deteriorated and even dilapidated, requiring major repairs for most structures. Further social shifts toward lower-status groups or minority groups occur. Property is now marketable only to the lowest socioeconomic groups capable of paying for it. Profitability of rental units declines and cash flows wane. More and more subsistence-level households move into and dominate the area. Pessimism about its future becomes widespread.

Stage 5 *Nonviable and heavily abandoned neighborhoods:* Neighborhoods of this type have reached a "terminal point" at which massive abandonment occurs, and expectations about the area's future are nil. Residents have the lowest social status and lowest incomes in the entire region; even they consider the area one to move away from.

The wording in the preceding five-stage description suggests that once a neighborhood is no longer at Stage 1, it can move only downward through subsequent stages, which is not true. Many neighborhood preservation programs have resulted in upward movement (such as changing a neighborhood from Stage 3 to Stage 2). Thus as shown in Figure 4–1, the five stages represent a continuum along which a neighborhood can move in either direction. Field research throughout the country suggests, however, that few neighborhoods improve significantly once they are well into Stage 3 and decline is clearly underway. As mentioned earlier, half stages (Stages 1.5, 2.5, 3.5, and 4.5) were also used in Cleveland so as to define the gradations of neighborhood change more narrowly and to facilitate the grouping of neighborhoods with the most similar characteristics.

Table 4–1 presents another description of the five general stages of neighborhood change in terms of specific conditions normally associated with each stage. This classification system rather closely reflects real estate market conditions. Stage 1 "healthy" neighborhoods exhibit rising prices, readily available conventional mortgages at "going rates," reputations as "good places to live" among persons who are not residents of the neighborhoods, and high levels of maintenance and repair. Neighborhoods in subsequent stages demonstrate progressive degrees of deviation from "normal" real estate market conditions. Typical indicators of market abnormality are: lack of mortgage availability (or use of government-insured loans exclusively), stable or declining property values, deferred or neglected maintenance, subdivision of large houses or apartments into a number of smaller units, high vacancy, vandalism, tax delinquency, and abandonment of buildings.

The patterns of socioeconomic changes in declining neighborhoods

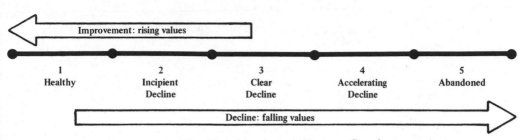

Figure 4–1. The Neighborhood Change Continuum.

Prepared by Real Estate Research Corporation

are quite consistent across the United States. For instance, average household income declines from Stage 2 to Stage 5, and elderly households tend to predominate in Stage 2 and then be replaced by larger, poorer families in Stage 3. Racial change often occurs during the neighborhood decline process, and tenancy usually shifts from predominantly owner occupancy to predominantly renter occupancy.

Most of the neighborhood stages just described exist in Cleveland. Only Stage 5, which is defined as "unhealthy and nonviable," is not apparent in any sizable area within the city. Because of Cleveland's effective demolition program, areas that might have been in Stage 5 a few years ago actually have been upgraded to Stage 4.5. The removal of vacant and vandalized buildings has improved the appearance of several inner-city areas and has also reduced the feelings of fear and foreboding of residents and visitors.

Based on a field inspection of Cleveland's neighborhoods and available data on population and housing characteristics, each statistical area within the city was classified by residential stage or status as shown in Figure 4–2. Because of their large size, the statistical areas used in this analysis are not all homogeneous neighborhoods. A statistical area that has been designated Stage 2, for example, may have small pockets of significantly better (Stage 1.5) or significantly worse (Stage 2.5) areas within it. Most of the areas are similar throughout, however, and can reasonably be placed in one category.

As illustrated in Figure 4–2, the most severely deteriorated neighborhoods are located in the section of Cleveland just east of downtown and the industrial valley. Deterioration has for the most part spread northeast from the West Central area, moving through East and West Hough toward the residential areas along Lake Erie on the eastern edge of the city. Within these three central neighborhoods are large amounts of vacant land. West Central, the area of greatest deterioration, has several

Table 4–1

Characteristics of Neighborhoods in the Five General Stages on the Change Continuum

Stage 1 Neighborhoods (Healthy and Viable)

New and growing area, or
Older area that is not changing.

Mostly families, some older couples, or
Mostly adults with few children.

Nearly everyone has moderate, middle or high income.

Mainly single family homes, but some apartments, or
Mainly apartments and townhouses.

Buildings well kept up; city services good.

Home prices and rents rising; neighborhood popular place to live in.

People feel safe in neighborhood.

Stage 2 Neighborhoods (Incipient Decline)

Older housing; more housing units.

Older families; more older people living alone.

People have somewhat lower incomes.

Older people in houses that are difficult to keep up; some houses divided into apartments, or
Families moving into apartments where only adults lived.

Stores and businesses appear in scattered locations; some homes and apartments used for businesses.

Home prices and rents stable or starting to fall.

Stage 3 Neighborhoods (Clear Decline)

Larger families, more children.

More houses being divided into smaller apartments; more renters, or
More people crowding in apartments.

More minority, ethnic or lower income persons. Some welfare families moving in.

Poor upkeep of buildings; city services declining.

Less pride in neighborhood.

Fewer landlords live in neighborhood.

Home prices dropping.

Mortgages and home loans hard to come by.

Some empty houses.

Stage 4 Neighborhoods (Heavy Decline)

Population starts to drop. Many stores close.

More and more low-income people. More families with only one parent.

Only poor people of minority groups are moving in.

More empty houses and apartments. Home prices falling steadily; rents do not cover costs.

Mortgages and home loans impossible to get except from mortgage companies and private owners.

Buildings not kept up at all. Broken windows and boarded-up buildings. Some vandalism.

Garbage not picked up as often. Streets dirty.

More people on welfare.

People afraid for their own safety.

Stage 5 Neighborhoods (Unhealthy and Nonviable)

People move out and others do not move in.

Buildings abandoned, vandalized. Many fires. Many buildings torn down. Many vacant areas.

All residents very poor.

No repairs made on outside of buildings. Garbage and bulk trash piles up.

Most people are afraid to go out of their buildings at night.

Only a few small, heavily guarded stores.

Source; Real Estate Research Corporation, *Neighborhood Preservation: A Catalog of Local Programs* (Washington, D.C.: U.S. Government Printing Office, 1975), p. 268.

urban renewal clearance projects within its boundaries and has the largest percentage of cleared land. Numerous buildings have also been demolished by the city in East and West Hough. Under the demolition program operating throughout the early 1970s, buildings in central Cleveland have been torn down soon after they have been abandoned or have become a safety hazard. About 60 percent of the delinquent parcels in West Hough are vacant, as are many other lots that have been cleared through urban renewal and the city's demolition program. If deteriorating or vandalized buildings remained on most of these parcels, the area would rank lower on the neighborhood change continuum.

Some of the other neighborhoods on Cleveland's East Side are in much better physical condition than the three core areas. For instance, immediately adjacent to downtown is a very stable, ethnic, working-class neighborhood. Although residential blocks in this neighborhood are scattered among industrial land uses, very little housing deterioration has occurred. Far northeastern and southeastern sections of the city have also experienced little physical decay.

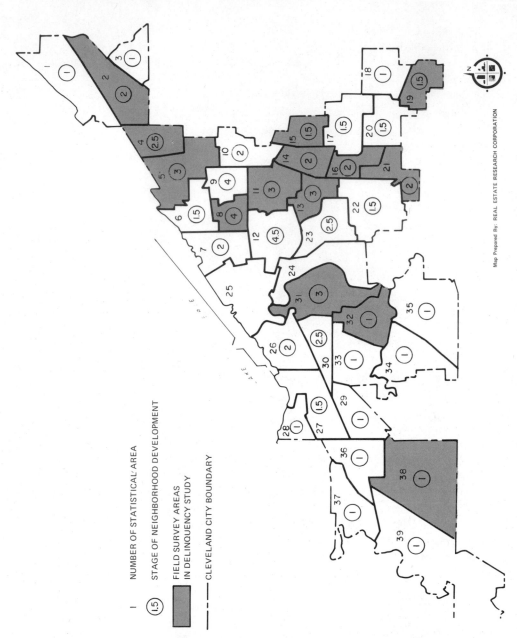

Figure 4–2. Stages of Neighborhood Development of City of Cleveland's Residential Areas.

Table 4–2
Selected Population, Housing, and Tax Delinquency Data for the City of Cleveland's Residential Statistical Areas

Statistical Area Name and Number	Median Household Income[a]	% of Housing Units Owner-Occupied in 1970	Number of Delin-quent Parcels in 1974	% of Total Parcels Delin-quent in 1974	Size of Sample in Surveyed Areas
Stage 1					
West					
Riverside (39)	$9,929	75.9%	115	1.7%	
Puritas-Bellaire-Longmead (38)	$10,157	84.9	294	3.0	50%
Munn-Warren (37)	$10,781	79.6	40	1.1	
Jefferson (36)	$9,518	68.7	107	1.5	
Broadview-Schaaf (35)	$9,085	66.8	145	2.0	
Memphis-Fulton (34)	$9,396	70.7	58	1.1	
Clark-Fulton (33)	$8,125	54.1	157	2.8	
Denison (32)	$7,641	45.9	133	2.8	30
Edgewater (28)	$7,560	27.6	53	2.8	
Midwest South (29)	$9,269	59.5	64	1.3	
East					
North Collinwood-Wildwood (1)	$8,757	55.9	201	2.9	
Euclid (3)	$8,830	42.9	51	2.5	
Harvard-Lee (18)	$11,970	96.3	170	3.5	
Stage 1.5					
West					
Midwest North (27)	$8,189	43.8	198	3.3	
East					
South Broadway (22)	$7,906	49.1	226	3.5	
Corlett (20)	$8,565	73.2	199	3.8	
Lee-Seville-Miles (19)	$9,844	81.1	334	13.0	
Mt. Pleasant (17)	$7,078	49.3	437	5.9	
Shaker Square (15)	$7,931	34.0	111	3.7	100
Norwood (6)	$6,252	35.8	352	8.3	
Stage 2					
West					
Near West Side (26)	$5,387	22.9	225	6.1	
East					
Miles-Warner (21)	$8,521	67.6	199	5.8	100
Paul Revere (16)	$7,974	66.1	188	5.7	100
Woodland Hills (14)	$6,528	40.4	168	5.4	100
University Circle (10)	$2,502	23.0	132	7.2	
Goodrich (7)	$5,762	25.7	97	4.1	
South Collinwood (2)	$7,844	45.4	260	5.2	50

Source: U.S. Census, 1970; Cleveland City Planning Commission.
[a]Median income figures for families and unrelated individuals.

Table 4–2 Continued

Statistical Area Name and Number	Median Household Income[a]	% of Housing Units Owner-Occupied in 1970	Number of Delin-quent Parcels in 1974	% of Total Parcels Delin-quent in 1974	Size of Sample in Surveyed Areas
Stage 2.5					
West					
Fulton-Train (30)	$7,214	36.3	224	5.5	
East					
North Broadway (23)	$7,554	51.0	167	4.4	
Forest Hills (4)	$7,629	41.2	355	6.7	100
Stage 3					
West					
Tremont (31)	$6,155	30.6	320	7.8	100
East					
Kinsman (13)	$3,928	22.4	361	22.7	25
East Central (11)	$3,926	22.5	1,090	21.9	25
Glenville (5)	$6,245	41.1	1,103	14.5	100
Stage 4					
East					
East Hough (9)	$3,862	19.1	764	21.0	
West Hough (8)	$3,377	16.6	1,015	32.0	100
Stage 4.5					
East					
West Central (12)	$3,196	8.0	998	23.4	

Cleveland's West Side differs distinctly from its East Side. Very few West Side neighborhoods have significant deterioration. One statistical area adjacent to the industrial valley is at Stage 3 on the neighborhood classification scale, but this relatively small pocket of deterioration is different in both quality and quantity from the neighborhood decline on the East Side. Much less housing abandonment and demolition have occurred, and deterioration is not widespread. The statistical area immediately west of downtown shows signs of incipient decline; however, this trend is being arrested by historic preservation and general housing rehabilitation efforts. The only other significant decline on the West Side is the result of land clearance for a proposed highway and the accompanying neglect of dwellings adjacent to the cleared land. Most West Side neighborhoods are stable, well-maintained, Stage 1 areas.

Population and Housing Characteristics

The conclusions we derived from our physical inspection of Cleveland's neighborhoods corresponded closely with socioeconomic differentiations among the areas. After preparing a preliminary categorization of the city's thirty-seven residential statistical areas according to Real Estate Research Corporation's continuum of neighborhood change, we analyzed housing and population data for the areas to determine whether sections of the city that had been classified in specific stages exhibited similar socioeconomic characteristics. The match was very good. In the few cases where socioeconomic data suggested a higher ranking than the physical inspection, the difference was attributable to rapid downward change since the 1970 Census, which was our primary source for population and housing information.

In evaluating the socioeconomic characteristics of neighborhoods at various stages, the following trends became apparent:

1. The stage of neighborhood change is closely tied to its residents' income. Beginning with relatively high income levels in Stage 1 areas, median incomes generally decrease in each successive stage of decline. The 1970 median household incomes in Stage 1 areas of Cleveland ranged from approximately $7500 to $12,000; whereas the median incomes were only at the $3000 to $4000 level in Stage 4 and 4.5 neighborhoods. There were a few exceptions to this trend. Some working-class neighborhoods with large ethnic concentrations had experienced much less physical deterioration than other areas with similar median household incomes. Goodrich, for example, had a 1970 median household income of only $5762, which was lower than the comparable figure for Tremont. Yet Goodrich has experienced relatively little physical deterioration and fits well into Stage 2, whereas Tremont is in Stage 3. (For more detail on the figures substantiating this trend and those described subsequently, see Tables A–1 to A–3 in Appendix A.)

2. Neighborhoods in late stages of decline have very high percentages of families receiving Aid to Dependent Children (ADC), whereas those areas in Stages 1 and 1.5 usually have low proportions of ADC families. Because the eligibility requirements for families receiving ADC were changed, it is difficult to analyze the increase in ADC families between 1970 and 1974. Areas that are just beginning to decline, however, appear to have had larger increases in the proportions of ADC families than either stable areas or most of the areas that had already experienced significant deterioration. This trend may be more apparent than real, resulting partly from the revised eligibility requirements that enabled more families to qualify for aid.

3. Seriously deteriorated neighborhoods frequently have larger minority group populations than stable, healthy areas. Neighborhood condition appears, however, to be tied more directly to income than to race. The relatively stable Stage 1 and 1.5 neighborhoods of Har-

vard-Lee and Lee-Seville-Miles, for instance, have black populations of greater than 90 percent and high median incomes. In contrast,
Tremont, a declining Stage 3 neighborhood, has a black population of
only 4 percent and a low median income, particularly in its most
severely deteriorated section adjacent to the industrial valley.

4. Another measure of the relative economic status of neighborhoods is
the median value of owner-occupied units. Median home value, like
median household income, is generally high in Stage 1 areas and
progressively lower in neighborhoods exhibiting more and more physical deterioration. The exception is working-class, ethnic neighborhoods in which housing values are traditionally low but stable.

5. The percentage of single-family homes among total residential structures varies greatly at the different stages of neighborhood change.
Neighborhoods in Stage 1 usually have very high percentages of
single-family units, whereas most substantially deteriorated areas
have relatively low percentages. Since multifamily units in declining
areas often deteriorate and are demolished first, it is likely that
single-family units made up an even smaller percentage of the housing
units in the late-stage areas before neighborhood decline began. Thus
although areas with small percentages of single-family units can remain healthy and viable over many decades, those areas are more
susceptible to decay than basically single-family residential areas.

6. In general, as is the case for single-family homes, the percentage of
owner-occupied units is high in stable neighborhoods and very low in
deteriorated areas. In evaluating the owner-occupancy data shown in
Table A–1, however, physical characteristics of the housing stock in
individual areas must be considered. Both Shaker Square and Norwood, for instance, have much lower percentages of owner-occupied
units than the other neighborhoods in Stage 1.5, but these areas have
relatively high percentages of two-family dwellings. Therefore
owner-occupancy is much more common in Shaker Square and Norwood structures than is apparent when only the number of owner-
occupied units is considered.

A few Cleveland statistical areas contain diverse neighborhoods that
cannot be neatly classified together in one stage of neighborhood development. Norwood, for example, is composed of a fairly stable,
working-class, ethnic area and a rapidly deteriorating, low-income area
bordering on East Hough. Although the statistical area as a whole is
classified as Stage 1.5, the part of the area near East Hough is at Stage 3.5.
To determine the extent to which the deteriorated section affected housing and population characteristics of the entire neighborhood, we
analyzed data for each census tract in the statistical area. Data for census

tracts in Norwood and in other diverse statistical areas generally supported the findings stated above on the relationship between physical condition and housing and population characteristics.

Tax Delinquency Trends in Residential Areas

An analysis of property tax delinquency data for Cleveland's statistical areas shows that increases in tax delinquency correspond closely with the consecutive stages of neighborhood decline. The percentage of parcels that are delinquent is significantly greater in clearly deteriorating and heavily deteriorated neighborhoods than in areas that are stable or just beginning to decline. More importantly, however, there appears to be a correlation between the progressive decline of neighborhoods and increases in the rate of tax delinquency.

In Cleveland's Stage 1 neighborhoods, very little tax delinquency has occurred, and the percentage of parcels certified delinquent each year remained fairly constant between 1950 and 1972. A representative example is Midwest South, a Stage 1 neighborhood on the West Side. Few delinquent parcels accumulated in Midwest South between 1950 and 1972, and delinquencies accounted for no more than 1.6 percent of the area's total parcels in any year.

More than half the delinquent parcels in Stage 1 neighborhoods in 1974 became delinquent during that year; in other words, most of the delinquencies were new. Over 32 percent were not yet certified as delinquent in the auditor's records in 1974, and it is likely that many of the parcels that were actually certified delinquent were redeemed by 1975. Although 308 parcels were certified delinquent in Stage 1 areas in 1973, for example, only 155 parcels were still delinquent in 1974.

Trends in tax delinquency in Stage 1.5 neighborhoods are similar to those in Stage 1 areas. The percentages of all parcels in areas that were delinquent were usually very low, and a high proportion of the delinquencies were recent and had not yet been certified. As just discussed, many of those parcels were probably no longer delinquent by 1975. Only one neighborhood in Stage 1.5—Lee-Seville-Miles—noticeably diverged from this pattern. This neighborhood had population and housing characteristics that placed it in the upper range of the category; yet as early as 1966, 15 percent of all parcels in the neighborhood were tax delinquent. (Other similar neighborhoods had much smaller percentages of delinquent parcels in each year for which we examined data.) Also, the percentage of delinquent parcels added each year in Lee-Seville-Miles was somewhat more erratic than in other Stage 1.5 areas. Although some delinquent parcels in this area are owned by Penn Central, the number is small and does not explain the unusual delinquency pattern. The existence of pockets of poverty in an otherwise stable, middle-income area may be the cause of higher delinquency rates in Lee-Seville-Miles.

In Stage 2 neighborhoods, the percentage of tax delinquent parcels—although still small—was increasing in the early 1970s. In about 1971 the percentage of parcels that became delinquent each year began to increase slightly. Similar trends occurred in Stage 2.5 areas. An increase in the rate at which properties became delinquent began even earlier in Stage 3 neighborhoods, starting about 1970. Consequently, the percentage of all parcels that were tax delinquent also increased, though there was considerable variation in total delinquencies among Stage 3 areas. Nearly 23 percent of the parcels in Kinsman and 22 percent of those in East Central were tax delinquent in 1974, as compared to about 15 percent and 8 percent in Glenville and Tremont, respectively.

Tax delinquencies began occurring much earlier in Stage 4 and 4.5 neighborhoods than in areas at earlier stages of decline. Even as long ago as 1965, significant numbers of parcels were delinquent in these neighborhood categories. In West Hough, for example, over 14 percent of the total parcels were delinquent in 1966. By 1974, as illustrated in Figure 4–3, the proportion had increased to 32 percent. The corresponding figures for East Hough and West Central were 21 percent and 23 percent, respectively.

An analysis of tax delinquency data for Cleveland's residential statistical areas shows that the level of delinquency is closely correlated with neighborhood stability. High rates of property tax delinquency are common in areas where the socioeconomic characteristics of the population have changed and large, low-income families have moved in, housing has deteriorated, and rental occupancy has increased. On the other hand, low rates of delinquency are evident in stable areas with middle- to upper-income residents, low unemployment, and high owner-occupancy.

Rates of tax delinquency rise as other signs of deterioration become evident; thus increases in tax delinquency began much earlier in areas that are now severely deteriorated than in neighborhoods that are just beginning to decline. The rapid spread of decline in Cleveland is clearly illustrated by the timing of increases in the rates of delinquency in neighborhoods classified at various stages. In the Stage 4 and 4.5 areas, high rates of tax delinquency were evident in the mid-1960s; in Stage 3 areas, the delinquency rate accelerated in 1970; in Stage 2 areas, a perceptible increase occurred in 1971. The loose housing market in the city caused by high outmigration has allowed deterioration to fan out quickly from the worst areas, especially on the East Side.

A partial cause of the extensive tax delinquency in Cleveland's heavily deteriorated areas may be the charges made to property owners for special municipal activities that are listed as property assessments. If

SOURCE: CLEVELAND CITY PLANNING COMMISSION.

Figure 4–3. Tax Delinquent Parcels, West Hough, 1974.

unpaid, such assessments are treated as tax delinquencies. Parcels with overdue special assessments for the costs of such activities as building demolition and vacant lot clean-up are included among the total tax delinquent properties. Although 60 percent of the parcels listed on the city's condemnation/demolition lists are already tax delinquent, according to Cleveland City Planning Commission tabulations, a portion of the remaining 40 percent may become delinquent if owners refuse to pay demolition costs. During Real Estate Research Corporation's interviews with large-scale property owners in central Cleveland, several people stated that they frequently stop paying taxes on vacant lots when special assessments for city clean-up activities are added. Because such city activities are required most often in substantially deteriorated areas, the impact of special assessments on tax delinquency is likely to be greatest there.

Neighborhoods Selected for the Survey

Fourteen of Cleveland's thirty-seven residential statistical areas were selected for the City Planning Commission's 1975 field survey of delinquent structures. As shown in Table 4–2 (pp. 75–76), the survey was conducted in two neighborhoods classified as being in Stage 1, two in Stage 1.5, four in Stage 2, one in Stage 2.5, four in Stage 3, and one in Stage 4. The only Stage 4.5 neighborhood in the city, West Central, was not included in the survey because of the preponderance of public housing and institutional uses in the area.

The fourteen areas surveyed contain slightly over one-half of Cleveland's tax delinquent parcels. Although emphasis was placed on areas where the delinquency problem was most serious, the selected survey areas were representative of all the city's neighborhood types (see Figure 4–2). Field researchers inspected approximately 3000 delinquent parcels; and in nine of the fourteen selected areas, they surveyed all the improved delinquent parcels. To reduce the amount of field work, they used 25-percent or 50-percent samples in the other five areas (see Table 4–2). We believe that a representative sample was achieved, and it is unlikely that a survey of additional parcels would have increased our knowledge significantly. Vacant delinquent parcels were not inspected because their basic character was already known. Also, their acquisition and management would pose fewer administrative problems than those of improved parcels if the foreclosure process were accelerated. In addition to the overall field survey, a special inventory was made in West Hough of all vacant parcels, whether or not they were delinquent.

Notes

1. Cleveland City Planning Commission, *Cleveland Housing Papers,* March 1973. See particularly "Poverty and Substandard Housing."

2. George Sternlieb and Robert W. Burchell, *Residential Abondonment: The Tenement Landlord Revisited* (New Brunswick, N.J.: Center for Urban Policy Research, 1973); George Sternlieb, *The Urban Housing Dilemma: The Dynamics of New York City's Rent Controlled Housing* (New York: Housing and Development Administration, 1972); George Sternlieb, Robert W. Lake, and Franklin J. James, *The Magnitude and Determinants of Property Tax Delinquency in Pittsburgh,* volume II (preliminary report prepared in 1974 for the city of Pittsburgh).

3. Public Affairs Counseling, a division of Real Estate Research Corporation, *The Dynamics of Neighborhood Change* (Washington, D.C.: U.S. Department of Housing and Urban Development, 1975).

4. The general pattern of urban development in the United States is described briefly at the beginning of Chapter 6.

5

Characteristics of Cleveland's Tax Delinquent Parcels

The Cleveland City Planning Commission's summer 1975 survey of tax delinquent parcels generated detailed information on nearly 6000 properties in fourteen representative residential statistical areas. Only parcels listed in the county auditor's records as having improvements on them were selected for physical inspection because the basic characteristics of vacant lots were, by definition, already known.[a] This field survey provided the factual basis for a profile of tax delinquent properties within the city. Some aspects of the profile were predictable; others were surprising and led to major modifications in the originally anticipated recommendations of the study.

Survey Methodology

As discussed in Chapter 4, the areas to be surveyed were selected after Cleveland's residential statistical areas had been classified by neighborhood condition. The sample was stratified according to stages of neighborhood development and the incidence of tax delinquency at each stage. By varying the sample size in individual statistical areas from 25 percent to 100 percent of all tax delinquent parcels, we were able to make the survey representative of citywide tax delinquency. Over one-half the delinquent improved parcels in Cleveland were covered by the survey, and their distribution in neighborhoods at differing stages of development closely approximates that of the full inventory of delinquent properties.

Prior to beginning the field inspections, City Planning Commission staff gathered basic data on each parcel in the survey. These data were derived from three key sources:

1. The Cuyahoga County Auditor's 1974 Billing Tape, which was the basis for selection of parcels and determination of the owner(s), location, and whether the property was improved. The 1974 tapes were prepared in December 1974, and the survey results reflect the status of the sampled properties in summer 1975.

---

[a] A separate vacant lot survey was conducted in West Hough to determine the amount of vacant land in that one inner-city statistical area. Both delinquent and nondelinquent parcels were covered in that survey, which provided the data for Figure 5–1.

2. *The 1969 Real Property Inventory*[b] which was used to determine the use of the improvements (for example, commercial, industrial, residential, institutional) and the number of units in individual structures. This source was consulted only for the delinquent parcels that were listed in the auditor's records as having improvements on them.

3. The 1974 Cleveland City Directory and the Cleveland Ohio Bell telephone book were checked to determine owner-occupancy. If the person listed as receiving the tax bill was also shown in either directory as residing at the address of the tax delinquent property, that person was assumed to be an owner-occupant.

During the field survey, data obtained from the auditor's billing tape and from the *Real Property Inventory* were checked for accuracy. Any indicated corrections were made in the field.

The field inspections involved driving through each survey neighborhood by car and locating the properties identified as improved on the 1974 auditor's billing tape. In the most deteriorated sections of the city where demolition has been extensive, Sanborn maps were often needed to locate addresses. The windshield survey of improved parcels was designed to determine the following:

1. Whether buildings had been demolished since the auditor's 1974 billing tape had been prepared
2. Whether buildings were occupied
3. Whether buildings were vandalized and/or open
4. Whether information obtained from the *1969 Real Property Inventory* on uses of structures and numbers of dwelling units appeared to be accurate
5. Whether exterior conditions of structures were comparable to, better than, or worse than those of other structures on the block.

The survey team was instructed to rate each building on two scales. The first involved ranking the exterior condition of the structure on a scale from 1 to 5 as follows:

1. Good condition
2. Signs of needed maintenance, but still in fairly good condition
3. Signs of obvious deterioration
4. Dilapidated (whether occupied or vacant)
5. Vacant, open, severely damaged by vandals, fire, and so forth

The second scale evaluated each building's exterior condition relative

---

[b]Published in Cleveland by the Real Property Inventory.

to that of other structures on the block. Both these ratings were obviously subjective. Prior to the field work, however, concerted attempts were made to control potential biases of the surveyors. The inspection team was given general criteria to consider in rating buildings, and supervisory staff visited representative neighborhoods with field team members to discuss the condition rankings.

During field inspections, the survey team was also requested to note the existence of any boarded-up buildings; fire-damaged buildings; posted condemnation signs on buildings; or posted FBI signs on buildings (indicating a Federal Housing Administration foreclosure).

All data obtained from source documents and through the field survey were placed on coded cards and then keypunched for computerized filing and subsequent analysis. Of the 2,959 parcels physically surveyed, complete information was gathered and recorded on 2923 properties.

Delinquent Property Survey Findings

The overall results of the Cleveland field survey, as extrapolated to the citywide total of tax delinquent properties, are shown in Table 5–1. Although we will discuss summary figures in more detail in subsequent sections of this chapter, we will mention several general findings here:

1. Forty percent of the tax delinquent properties in the city of Cleveland consisted of vacant lots. This is a higher proportion than the county auditor's records indicated, because field inspections in mid-1975 disclosed demolitions that had not yet been posted in county records. Thus 4400 of the city's over 11,000 delinquent parcels were vacant, unimproved properties.
2. Forty-six percent (5100) of the tax delinquent properties were occupied residential structures, half of them containing two or more units.
3. Nearly 40 percent of the occupied residential structures that were tax delinquent were owner-occupied. Thus 2000 of the 11,100 delinquent parcels in the city were the primary residences of the property owners, a much higher proportion than we expected.
4. Only 700 properties (6 percent of the total delinquent parcels in the city) contained occupied nonresidential structures.
5. Nine hundred tax delinquent parcels had vacant buildings on them. Most of these were residential properties.

The proportions of these five types of tax delinquent properties in neighborhoods at differing stages of development are shown in Table 5– 1.

Table 5–1
Characteristics of Delinquent Parcels in the City of Cleveland, by Stage of Neighborhood Development

Property Type	% of Total Delinquent Parcels by Neighborhood Stage						Number	% of Total Delinquent Parcels
	1	1.5	2	2.5	3	4–4.5		
Vacant lots	37%	27%	34%	41%	38%	54%	4,400	40%
Vacant buildings	4	8	9	8	11	7	900	8
Occupied non-residential structures	7	7	8	6	8	3	700	6
Renter-occupied residential structures	18	34	33	29	28	27	3,100	28
Owner-occupied residential structures	34	24	16	16	15	9	2,000	18
Total	100%	100%	100%	100%	100%	100%	11,100[a]	100%

Source: Extrapolation from Cleveland City Planning Commission Field Survey.
[a]Total is rounded and excludes delinquent properties in the downtown and the industrial valley.

Vacant Delinquent Parcels

As mentioned previously, the field survey revealed that 40 percent of the approximately 11,100 delinquent parcels in Cleveland (excluding the downtown and industrial valley areas) were vacant and unimproved. This percentage represented a very significant increase over the 1966 figure. Then, as shown in Table 5–2, only 23 percent of the delinquent parcels within the city were vacant lots. The tremendous increase in the proportion in eight years reflects the extensive abandonment and demolition that have occurred in many of Cleveland's East Side neighborhoods.

Not surprisingly, the percentage of vacant delinquent parcels is highest in the most deteriorated neighborhoods. In Stage 4 and 4.5 residential areas, approximately 54 percent of the delinquent parcels were unimproved in 1975. In contrast, only 37 percent of all delinquent parcels in Stage 1 neighborhoods and 27 percent of those in Stage 1.5 areas were vacant lots. The number, as well as the percentage, of vacant delinquent parcels also increased most rapidly between 1966 and 1975 in the heavily deteriorated neighborhoods.

Although survey information on all neighborhoods at each stage of development was not available, Table 5–2 shows the percentage of vacant

Table 5–2
Percent of Delinquent Parcels in the City of Cleveland and Selected Statistical Areas That Are Vacant

Statistical Area Name and Number	1966	1970	1975[a]
City of Cleveland	23%	29%	40%
Stage 1			
Denison (32)	37	33	29
Stage 1.5			
Shaker Square (15)	14	14	11
Stage 2			
South Collinwood (2)	26	23	29
Stage 2.5			
Glenville (5)	9	14	28
Stage 3			
Kinsman (13)	13	29	47
Stages 4 and 4.5			
West Hough (8)	10	31	58

Source: Cuyahoga County Auditor's records for 1966 and 1970; Cleveland City Planning Commission field survey for 1975.
[a] The 1975 figures are a result of physical inspections that revealed more vacant lots than were shown on the auditor's tapes. Because such surveys were not made in 1966 and 1970, the figures in the three columns may not be exactly comparable.

delinquent parcels in one statistical area at each stage on the neighborhood change continuum. In West Hough, a Stage 4 area, the percentage of delinquent parcels that were vacant increased from only 10 percent in 1966 to nearly 60 percent in 1975. In the Stage 1 neighborhood of Denison, however, the percentage of vacant delinquent parcels actually declined steadily—from 37 percent in 1966 to 33 percent in 1970 and 29 percent in 1975. In Glenville, which was at Stage 2.5 in 1975 and had been declining rapidly, the percentage of delinquent properties that were vacant tripled in nine years, rising from 9 percent in 1966 to 28 percent in 1975.

In the inner-city neighborhoods where housing deterioration and abandonment are most severe, large percentages of all parcels are vacant. The Cleveland City Planning Commission conducted a survey of all vacant properties in West Hough; its results are shown graphically in Figure 5–1. Although 32 percent of all parcels in West Hough were delinquent at the end of 1974 and 58 percent of those were vacant, there were many nondelinquent vacant parcels as well. An even greater share of the Stage 4.5 area of West Central consists of vacant delinquent and nondelinquent parcels. In all the Stage 4 and 4.5 neighborhoods together, one-half the delinquent acreage is vacant. This land has almost no market value, and the short-term reuse potential is negligible. The large numbers of nondelinquent vacant lots in these areas may result, in part, from delays in certification of the city's demolition costs as tax liens. Nonetheless, it appears that many owners of vacant lots are willing to invest limited amounts to retain control of their properties. Annual property taxes on a vacant parcel can amount to less than $35.

The high percentage of vacant delinquent and nondelinquent parcels in Stage 3 to 4.5 areas resulted in large part from the city demolishing condemned structures. Almost 60 percent of the parcels on Cleveland's 1974 Condemnation/Demolition lists were tax delinquent. Even more importantly, and somewhat surprisingly, over 50 percent of the delinquent structures razed in 1974 had been delinquent for only one to two years, as shown in Table 5–3. This fact conforms to comments made by large-scale, inner-city property-owners interviewed for this study. As discussed in Chapter 6, such landlords claimed that they usually did not stop paying taxes until they were ready to abandon their properties. The high percentage of buildings that were delinquent for only a short time before being demolished suggests that many property-owners pay their taxes up to the time of abandonment. Demolition generally does not occur for at least six months to a year after abandonment.

Unoccupied Delinquent Buildings

Approximately 900 parcels, or 8 percent of all tax delinquent parcels in Cleveland, had unoccupied improvements on them in mid-1975. Approx-

SOURCE: CLEVELAND CITY PLANNING COMMISSION.

Figure 5–1. Inventory of Vacant and Cleared Properties, West Hough, 1975.

Table 5–3
Tax Delinquent Parcels on the City of Cleveland's 1974 Demolition List

Tax Year Certified Delinquent	Number of Delinquent Parcels on Demolition List[a]	% of Parcels on Demolition List
Delinquent but not yet certified	56	14.0%
1974	106	26.4
1973	58	14.5
1972	31	7.7
1970–1971	55	13.7
1965–1969	66	16.5
Prior to 1965	29	7.2
Total	401	100.0%

Source: Cleveland City Planning Commission.

[a]Parcels in the demolition file as of November 27, 1974 were checked for delinquency on the 1974 Tax Duplicate. The 1974 duplicate is prepared at the end of the 1974 calendar year.

imately 37 percent of the unoccupied buildings in the field survey were open and vandalized and presumably awaiting demolition. Many of the other vacant buildings are likely to be in the same condition before long.

The neighborhoods with the highest percentages of unoccupied buildings were in Stage 3 on the neighborhood change continuum. As shown in Table 5–4, 11 percent of the delinquent parcels in Stage 3 areas contained unoccupied buildings. Neighborhoods classified as being both higher and

Table 5–4
Condition of Unoccupied Structures on Surveyed Tax Delinquent Properties, by Stage of Neighborhood Development

Neighborhood Stage		Vacant Buildings	
	% of Total Delinquent Parcels[a]	% Open and Vandalized	% Not Vandalized
Stage 1	4%	0%	100%
Stage 1.5	8	16	84
Stage 2	9	20	80
Stage 2.5	8	35	65
Stage 3	11	38	62
Stage 4	7	56	44
Total survey	—	37%	63%

Source: Cleveland City Planning Commission field survey.

[a]Information in this column is extrapolated from the sample to all neighborhoods at each stage in the city of Cleveland. Since the survey covered only improved parcels, the percentage of sampled delinquent parcels that are vacant buildings is much higher than the percent of all delinquent parcels in the neighborhoods that contain vacant buildings.

lower on the scale had fewer delinquent parcels with unoccupied structures. Stable areas in Stage 1 of neighborhood development generally
have very few unoccupied tax delinquent buildings. According to our
survey, none of the unoccupied buildings in neighborhoods of this type
was open and vandalized. Although the percentage of delinquent parcels
containing vacant buildings remained fairly constant for neighborhood
Stages 1.5 through 2.5, the proportion of vacant buildings that were open
and vandalized increased steadily with progressive neighborhood decline.
The figures in Table 5–4 show that 35 percent of the surveyed unoccupied
improvements in Stage 2.5 neighborhoods, and 38 percent of those in
Stage 3 areas, were open and vandalized. In these areas, visible housing
deterioration and structural abandonment were becoming increasingly
serious. The Stage 4 areas surveyed had small percentages of vacant
buildings, reflecting high demolition activity and large numbers of vacant
delinquent lots. However, a high percentage of the vacant buildings that
did exist in Stage 4 areas (56 percent) were open and vandalized.

Very few of the buildings that were vacant at the time of the survey
had been owner-occupied residential structures immediately prior to vacancy. None of the buildings in Stage 1 to 2 neighborhoods and less than 1
percent in Stage 2.5 to 4 areas were owner-occupied residences right
before they were vacated. This accords with findings in other cities that
abandonment of rental buildings is far more prevalent than that of
owner-occupied structures.

According to the field survey findings shown in Table 5–5, about 78
percent of the sample parcels with unoccupied structures contained residential units, or had contained them before vandalism or fire. In the areas
surveyed, which were primarily residential, another 18 percent of the
unoccupied sampled properties had been entirely in commercial use.

Table 5–5
**Surveyed Delinquent Parcels Containing Unoccupied Structures, by Use
of Structure**

Use of Structure	% of Total Sample Properties with Unoccupied Structures
Residential	71.1%
Mixed residential and commercial	7.1
Commercial	18.0
Industrial	2.6
Public utility	0.0
Institutional	1.2
Total unoccupied sample properties	100.0%

Source: Cleveland City Planning Commission field survey.

Occupied Delinquent Buildings

More than half of Cleveland's tax delinquent parcels contained occupied structures in 1975. As shown earlier in Table 5–1, about 5800 parcels, or 52 percent of all delinquent parcels in the city's residential neighborhoods, were improved with occupied buildings.^c Only 6 percent of the delinquent parcels contained occupied nonresidential structures, and the remainder—about 46 percent—were owner- and renter-occupied residential structures. (The unextrapolated survey results on vacant and improved parcels are presented in Appendix A, Table A–4.)

Only about 3 percent of the occupied, improved, delinquent parcels in Stage 4 and 4.5 neighborhoods contained commercial structures. In these seriously deteriorated neighborhoods, few businesses remained in either tax delinquent or nondelinquent buildings. On the other hand, Stage 3 areas, where decline was underway but not as advanced, had a large proportion of occupied delinquent structures in nonresidential uses. In Stage 3 areas, increasing numbers of low-income residents often result in decline of commercial strips and neighborhood convenience stores. The relatively high percentages of delinquent nonresidential buildings in the survey may be indicative of increasing financial problems among local businesses.

In 1975 in the city of Cleveland, most delinquent improved parcels (approximately 5100) contained occupied residential buildings. Such structures constituted a larger proportion of the delinquent parcels in stable neighborhoods than in heavily deteriorated ones. As indicated in Table 5–6, for example, 55 percent of the delinquent parcels in Stage 1 and 1.5 areas had occupied residential buildings, as compared to only 36 percent in Stage 4 and 4.5 neighborhoods. This is mainly because of the increasing percentages of vacant parcels in the deteriorating areas. The absolute number of delinquent occupied residential structures was greater in clearly declining and heavily deteriorated neighborhoods than in stable ones.

Housing Units in Occupied Structures

The proportion of delinquent parcels containing occupied residential structures becomes more obviously significant when expressed in terms of housing units. There were more than 10,050 housing units in occupied delinquent structures in the city of Cleveland in 1975. This modest estimate probably somewhat understates the actual number because it is

---

^cA building was listed as occupied if, in the judgment of the survey team, at least one unit was occupied. Thus actual occupancy rates in delinquent buildings are not known.

Table 5–6
Percent of Delinquent Parcels That Contain Occupied Residential
Structures, by Stage of Neighborhood Development

Neighborhood Stage	Occupied Residential Structures
Stage 1	52%
Stage 1.5	58
Stage 2	49
Stage 2.5	45
Stage 3	43
Stages 4–4.5	36
City of Cleveland	46%

Source: Cleveland City Planning Commission field survey.

based only on units in entirely residential structures and does not include units in structures with mixed residential and commercial uses. Depending on the occupancy rates in the delinquent structures, up to 4.5 percent of the city's households could be affected by the foreclosure process. About 54 percent of the tax delinquent housing units were located in clearly declining (Stage 3) and heavily deteriorated (Stage 4 and 4.5) neighborhoods, so many of the households occupying them would have low incomes.

Size of Occupied Residential Structures

Nearly 85 percent of all occupied residential structures in the city of Cleveland that were tax delinquent in 1975 were single-family dwellings or duplexes. As shown in Table 5–7, 49 percent of the occupied residential structures surveyed were single-family homes; another 35 percent were duplexes. Only about 5 percent of the occupied structures were apartment buildings containing five or more units. In Stage 1 areas, which include the newest sections of the city, most occupied delinquent structures (84 percent) were single-family homes. Over 96 percent of the structures with overdue taxes in Stage 1.5 areas had only one or two units; the proportions of single-family homes and duplexes were about equal. Even in heavily deteriorated Stage 4 neighborhoods, more than 70 percent of the delinquent residential structures were one- and two-unit buildings.

Very few large apartment buildings were tax delinquent in mid-1975, for probably three principal reasons:

1. Cleveland has always had a smaller proportion of large than small residential structures. Most of the city's housing units consist of single-family homes and duplexes.

Table 5-7

Size Distribution of Occupied Residential Structures Surveyed, by Stage of Neighborhood Development

Neighborhood Stage	One-Unit Structures	Two-Unit Structures	Three- to Four-Unit Structures	Five- or More Unit Structures
	% of Total Occupied Structures[a]			
Stage 1	83.8%	13.2%	1.5%	1.5%
Stage 1.5	49.6	46.8	3.6	0.0
Stage 2	52.6	41.5	4.1	1.8
Stage 2.5	44.5	31.3	15.4	8.8
Stage 3	50.7	33.9	10.9	4.5
Stage 4	36.5	34.5	17.1	11.9
Total survey	49.2%	35.3%	10.2%	5.3%

Source: Cleveland City Planning Commission field survey.

[a]No information was available on the number of units in about 4 percent of the occupied residential structures in the sample.

2. The proportion of large residential structures in the city has been decreasing. In most of the nation's large central cities, residential abandonment has occurred first in marginally profitable, old multi-family buildings, which are susceptible to rapid deterioration as neighborhoods decline and lower- and lower-income, often large, families move in.[d] Although the survey data in Cleveland do not show this pattern of neighborhood deterioration, the process probably took place much earlier in the older, inner-city neighborhoods that were already heavily deteriorated by 1975. It is likely that many of the large apartment buildings became delinquent and were abandoned and demolished several years before the survey. By 1975 those parcels, if delinquent, would have been in the categories of vacant or unoccupied improved parcels.

3. A number of the remaining large apartment buildings in central Cleveland, especially those on the East Side, are owned by large-scale landlords. As is discussed in Chapter 6, many of these owners pay

---

[d]In his study of New York City's rent-controlled housing, George Sternlieb pointed out the particular "vulnerability of multi-unit structures to the behavior of a single tenant or to the disabilities originating in a single apartment." Sternlieb observes that, in small one- and two-unit structures, the destruction caused by a problem tenant (such as stripped water pipes or broken heating equipment) is limited to one or two units. In a multifamily structure, on the other hand, numerous households can be victimized by activity in one apartment. Thus large multifamily buildings are much more vulnerable to deterioration, and they decrease in number more rapidly than smaller residential structures. See George Sternlieb, *The Urban Housing Dilemma: The Dynamics of New York City's Rent Controlled Housing* (New York: Housing and Development Administration, 1972), p. 614

taxes on their buildings as long as they continue managing them. Thus large residential structures that are tax delinquent tend to be abandoned and vacant rather than occupied.

Units in duplexes would be affected by changes in the foreclosure process more than those in any other type of residential structure. Table 5–8 shows that about one-third of all housing units in delinquent structures in Cleveland were in duplexes. Because owners of duplexes can live in one unit and rent out the other, they often have greater financial staying power than owners of single-family homes or purely rental buildings. Thus the number of duplexes in Cleveland has probably added stability to the housing market, though the high rate of delinquency now indicates that many duplex owners are in financial trouble. Another 23 percent of the units in delinquent structures were single-family homes. Together, units in one- and two-unit structures accounted for about 56 percent of all delinquent housing units in 1975. Only about 27 percent of the units were in multifamily structures with more than four apartments.

Occupancy of Residential Structures

More than one-third of Cleveland's tax delinquent occupied residential structures (2000) are owner-occupied. As was shown in Table 5–1, the proportion of owner-occupied residential parcels in relation to total delinquent properties decreases rapidly as neighborhoods begin to decline.

Table 5–8

Number of Units in Delinquent Occupied Residential Structures Surveyed, by Stage of Neighborhood Development

	% of Occupied Units[a]			
Neighborhood Stage	One-Unit Structures	Two-Unit Structures	Three- to Four- Unit Structures	Five- or More Unit Structures
Stage 1	65.5%	20.7%	4.6%	9.2%
Stage 1.5	31.8	59.8	8.4	0.0
Stage 2	31.5	49.6	8.5	10.4
Stage 2.5	16.6	23.4	20.1	39.9
Stage 3	24.6	33.0	18.6	23.8
Stage 4	12.6	23.9	20.7	42.8
Total survey	23.1%	33.2%	17.0%	26.7%

Source: Cleveland City Planning Commission field survey.

[a]No information was available on the number of units in about 4 percent of the occupied residential structures in the sample.

Homeowners who can afford to move often do so as uncertainty develops about the future of a residential area. The remaining owner-occupants tend to be either older persons whose homes are paid for but who could not afford to make monthly payments on a new mortgage or new buyers who could not afford higher priced homes.

The departure of owner-occupants is unfortunate, because their continued presence generally has a positive impact on the surrounding area. Units occupied by their owners are usually better maintained than those rented by absentee owners. Owner-occupants have a vested interest in their communities and tend to be more actively involved in neighborhood organizations and in encouraging continued provision of adequate or improved public and private services to their areas.

Homeowners may be tax delinquent for a number of reasons. Some may be experiencing temporary financial difficulties as a result of sickness, divorce, loss of employment, etc. Elderly homeowners who are unaware of the homestead exemption may find themselves without sufficient funds to pay their taxes. (The homestead exemption reduces property taxes for homeowners over 65 years of age in proportion to their incomes.) Some new buyers purchasing homes on land contracts are reportedly unaware that back taxes remain unpaid—and therefore that foreclosure may be threatened. Other homeowners may be discouraged from investing further in their properties because of the declining values of their houses and their loss of equity. Some of the owners simply have incomes that are inadequate to support their properties.

Nearly 60 percent of all delinquent owner-occupied parcels were located in relatively stable Stage 1 to 2 areas, and a high proportion of those delinquencies could be expected to have been caused by temporary financial problems and therefore to be relatively short-term. As shown in Table 5–9, only 13 percent of the delinquent owner-occupied parcels were in severely deteriorated Stage 4 and 4.5 areas. However, 22 percent were located in Stage 3 neighborhoods. In those areas, where physical deterioration and declining housing values were becoming apparent, many owners might be unwilling to make further investments in their houses— even if faced with rapid foreclosure procedures. This would be especially likely if taxes had been delinquent for some time and a large bill had accumulated.

Approximately 2,100 parcels, or 28 percent of all delinquent parcels in the city of Cleveland, contained renter-occupied structures in the 1974–1975 period. The percentage of delinquent parcels with renter-occupied structures was lowest (18 percent) in very stable Stage 1 neighborhoods, as was shown in Table 5–1. It was significantly higher about 33 percent) in less stable, Stage 1.5 and 2 areas, but it declined slowly in each successive neighborhood stage to 27 percent of all parcels

Table 5–9
Distribution of Delinquent, Owner- and Renter-Occupied Structures, by
Stage of Neighborhood Development

Neighborhood Stage	% of Total Delinquent, Owner-Occupied Structures	% of Total Delinquent, Renter-Occupied Structures
Stage 1	27%	9%
Stage 1.5	22	20
Stage 2	10	13
Stage 2.5	6	7
Stage 3	22	27
Stages 4–4.5	13	24
Total	100%	100%

Source: Extrapolation from Cleveland City Planning Commission field survey.

in Stage 4 and 4.5 areas. This gradual drop in the percentage of delinquent parcels containing renter-occupied structures is largely attributable to the parallel increase in the proportion of delinquent vacant lots in more deteriorated neighborhoods. Actually, rental occupancy becomes much more prevalent than owner occupancy in areas at late stages of decline.

In Cleveland's Stage 1 neighborhoods, twice as many owner-occupied properties were delinquent as renter-occupied ones. In large part, this reflects the predominance of owner-occupied, single-family homes in the housing stock of the city's newer areas. Stage 2, 2.5, and 3 neighborhoods exhibited the opposite delinquency pattern: The percentage of delinquent renter-occupied buildings was twice as high as that for owner-occupied buildings. Three times as many rental structures as owner-occupied ones were delinquent in the Stage 4 and 4.5 neighborhoods. As shown in the distribution in Table 5–9, approximately half the delinquent, renter-occupied structures were located in declining and heavily deteriorated Stage 3 to 4.5 areas. This is partly because these older areas always had a significant proportion of rental housing units. However, it is also because many homeowners have already moved out, absentee ownership has become more common, and a higher proportion of the remaining structures (though still by no means a majority) are owned by large-scale landlords.

In total, over 60 percent of all the delinquent occupied structures in Cleveland were renter-occupied. As illustrated by the figures in Table 5–10, the percentage of renter-occupied delinquent structures was lowest in Stage 1 areas (35 percent of all occupied delinquent residential buildings) and then increased steadily to 74 percent of the occupied residential structures in Stage 4.5 neighborhoods. A comparison of the percentages in Tables 5–10 and 5–11 shows that the pattern of delinquent

Table 5–10
Percent of Delinquent Occupied Residential Structures That Were Renter-Occupied in 1975

Neighborhood Stage	Delinquent, Renter-Occupied Structures as % of Occupied Structures
Stage 1	35%
Stage 1.5	59
Stage 2	67
Stage 2.5	65
Stage 3	65
Stages 4–4.5	74

Source: Extrapolated from Cleveland City Planning Commission field survey.

parcels in terms of tenure is very similar to the overall ownership pattern in the neighborhoods at various stages of decline, as reported in the 1970 Census. The figures in Table 5–10 are for structures, whereas those in Table 5–11 are for units and therefore could be expected to be higher because most rental units are in multifamily buildings. In the early decline neighborhoods (Stages 1.5 to 2.5), a disproportionate number of rental buildings appear to have been tax delinquent, which suggests that disinvestment was more prevalent among landlords than among owner-occupants.

Condition of Occupied Delinquent Structures

The exterior condition of most occupied tax delinquent structures was similar to that of adjacent buildings. As shown in Table 5–12, only 14.2 percent of all occupied delinquent structures appeared to be in worse

Table 5–11
Percent of All Housing Units That Were Renter-Occupied in 1970

Neighborhood Stage	Renter-Occupied Units as % of Total Occupied Housing Units
Stage 1	37%
Stage 1.5	48
Stage 2	58
Stage 2.5	57
Stage 3	71
Stages 4–4.5	85

Source: U.S. Bureau of the Census.

Table 5-12
Relative and Absolute Physical Condition of Total Occupied Delinquent Structures

All Types of Structures	Relative Condition			Absolute Condition			
	Better than Adjacent Buildings	Same as Adjacent Buildings	Worse than Adjacent Buildings	1—Good Condition	2—Fairly Good Condition	3—Deterioration Apparent	4—Dilapidated
Stage 1	3.3%	88.9%	7.8%	30.3%	57.3%	12.4%	0.0%
Stage 1.5	1.3	90.5	8.2	29.2	62.6	7.6	0.6
Stage 2	4.8	89.0	6.2	16.4	67.0	16.4	0.2
Stage 2.5	6.0	79.6	14.4	11.6	66.6	20.9	0.9
Stage 3	11.0	72.8	16.2	16.4	56.1	25.7	1.8
Stage 4	16.7	61.3	22.0	9.3	67.5	22.6	0.6
Total survey	9.3	76.5	14.2	16.3	61.4	21.2	1.1
Residential structures[a]	9.2	76.1	14.7	15.7	60.3	21.9	1.1
Mixed Residential and commercial structures	3.2	87.1	9.7	3.6	76.8	19.6	0.0
Commercial structures	9.2	79.9	10.9	12.8	69.7	16.3	1.2

Source: Cleveland City Planning Commission field survey.
[a]For a detailed breakdown of occupied residential buildings by neighborhood stage, see Appendix A, Table A-5.

condition than surrounding buildings at the time of the 1975 field survey. Neither residential structures, mixed residential and commercial structures, nor strictly commercial buildings were frequently in worse condition than adjacent structures. The proportion of occupied, delinquent structures that were in the same condition as adjacent structures declined, however, from 88.9 percent in Stage 1 areas to 61.3 percent in Stage 4 neighborhoods. In the latter areas, significantly higher percentages of delinquent structures were either better or worse than adjacent buildings.

The field survey indicated that very few (only 1.1 percent) occupied delinquent structures appeared dilapidated, while nearly 78 percent of the occupied buildings were at least in fairly good condition. It is possible that the data in Table 5–12 were biased somewhat by the attitudes of survey team members. Deteriorating structures in Stage 1.5 areas, for example, might have been evaluated more critically than similar buildings in Stage 4 areas. Overall, however, we believe that the data on structural condition were recorded fairly accurately. Most of the relative and absolute rankings are consistent, and the differences for occupied, vacant, and owner-occupied buildings appear reasonable. We should stress, though, that the condition rankings were based on *exterior* inspections only. These buildings may have had more substantial interior or structural deficiencies.

The physical deterioration of delinquent structures was found to be closely linked to the stages of neighborhood change. Although more than 30 percent of the occupied structures in Stage 1 areas were in good condition, only about 9 percent of those in Stage 4 neighborhoods fell into that category. The proportion of occupied buildings in "fairly good" condition was remarkably constant in all stages. However, the percentages of deteriorated and dilapidated buildings increased in successive stages of neighborhood decline. Only 12 percent of the occupied structures in Stage 1 areas had visible deterioration, whereas about 25 percent of the buildings in Stage 3 and 4 areas were deteriorated or dilapidated. Because most smaller residential buildings in Cleveland are of wood frame construction, they can deteriorate rapidly if they are left vacant, or even if normal maintenance is neglected.

Not surprisingly, owner-occupied structures were more frequently in better relative and absolute physical condition than residential structures (both renter- and owner-occupied) in general. More than 11 percent of the owner-occupied structures, as compared with 9 percent of all occupied residential structures, were in better condition than adjacent buildings; and 23 percent of the owner-occupied dwellings versus 17 percent of all residential buildings were in good condition. As was found among all other types of structures, the percentage of owner-occupied buildings that were in good physical condition declined with successive stages of neighborhood change. Although about 33 percent of the owner-occupied structures in Stage 1 areas were in good condition, only 13 percent of this category of buildings in Stage 4 areas were similarly well maintained. In most areas, though, these proportions were higher than those for residential structures in general. Except in clearly deteriorating and heavily deteriorated neighborhoods, owner-occupied structures were seldom dilapidated. The condition data for owner-occupied residences in the Cleveland delinquency survey are shown in Table 5–13.

The perhaps surprising results on the relatively good exterior condition of the occupied buildings surveyed may reflect the fact that abandonment results from neighborhood blight and declining socioeconomic conditions much more than from structural deterioration. When structures actually become dilapidated, they are more likely to lose tenants, who can usually find somewhat better quality housing in loose inner-city housing markets. Buildings that lose numerous tenants, or at least most of the reliable tenants, quickly become financial liabilities and are abandoned by owners. As the last tenants depart, vandals begin their destruction. Thus the number of seriously deteriorated vacant buildings is high and in large part constitutes a predemolition inventory.

Condition of Vacant Delinquent Buildings

Severe deterioration was much more common among vacant than occupied delinquent buildings. Nearly 10 percent of the vacant delinquent structures were dilapidated, and almost one-third were open and vandalized. In addition, they were quite often more deteriorated than adjacent buildings. Table 5–14 shows that almost 70 percent of the residential and 54 percent of the mixed residential and commercial structures were in worse condition than surrounding buildings.

Vacant, delinquent structures in the more deteriorated neighborhoods were more likely to be in poor condition. Stage 1 areas had a very small proportion of vacant buildings (4 percent); and according to the survey, 60 percent of those structures were in fairly good condition. In Stage 1.5 to 4.5 areas, where there were more vacant buildings, the percentages of vacant structures that were dilapidated or open and vandalized increased with each successive neighborhood stage. The percentages of vacant buildings in these two categories were as follows:

Stage 1.5	Stage 2	Stage 2.5	Stage 3	Stages 4–4.5
15.8%	16.3%	29.0%	46.5%	66.2%

Multiparcel Delinquent Property Owners

The number of Cleveland property owners with five or more delinquent improved parcels was small. Only 51 owners had five or more such

Table 5–13
Relative and Absolute Physical Condition of Owner-Occupied Delinquent Structures

All Types of Structures	Relative Condition			Absolute Condition			
	Better than Adjacent Buildings	Same as Adjacent Buildings	Worse than Adjacent Buildings	1—Good Condition	2—Fairly Good Condition	3—Deterioration Apparent	4—Dilapidated
Stage 1	3.7%	85.2%	11.1%	33.3%	48.2%	18.5%	0.0%
Stage 1.5	0.0	96.6	3.4	32.8	63.8	3.4	0.0
Stage 2	7.9	86.8	5.3	16.7	68.4	14.0	0.9
Stage 2.5	10.6	78.8	10.6	21.5	58.5	20.0	0.0
Stage 3	14.3	70.4	15.3	23.3	55.4	19.3	2.0
Stage 4	20.8	48.0	31.2	13.2	57.9	26.3	2.6
Total survey	11.5%	74.9%	13.6%	22.5%	58.4%	17.7%	1.4%

Source: Cleveland City Planning Commission field survey.

Table 5–14
Relative and Absolute Physical Condition of Total Vacant Delinquent Structures

All Types of Structures	Relative Condition			Absolute Condition				
	Better than Adjacent Buildings	Same as Adjacent Buildings	Worse than Adjacent Buildings	1—Good Condition	2—Fairly Good Condition	3—Deterioration Apparent	4—Dilapidated	5—Open and Vandalized
Stage 1	0.0%	60.0%	40.0%	0.0%	60.0%	40.0%	0.0%	0.0%
Stage 1.5	0.0	36.8	63.2	0.0	26.3	57.9	0.0	15.8
Stage 2	0.0	65.3	34.7	10.2	42.9	30.6	10.2	6.1
Stage 2.5	0.0	48.4	51.6	0.0	35.5	35.5	12.8	16.2
Stage 3	0.6	34.6	54.8	1.3	18.9	33.3	9.4	37.1
Stage 4	3.9	15.8	80.3	4.1	18.9	10.8	10.8	55.4
Total survey	1.2	36.6	62.2	3.0	24.9	29.7	9.5	32.9
Residential structures[a]	1.2	28.9	69.9	2.1	19.2	27.1	13.3	38.3
Mixed residential and commercial structures	0.0	45.8	54.2	0.0	20.8	41.7	12.5	25.0
Commercial structures	1.7	63.3	35.0	1.7	46.6	40.0	1.7	10.0

Source: Cleveland City Planning Commission field survey.

[a]For a detailed breakdown of vacant residential buildings by neighborhood stage, see Appendix A, Table A–6.

properties within the city, and these owners accounted for only 480 structures (approximately 8 percent of all improved delinquent parcels). A small number of owners controlled a larger number of vacant delinquent parcels, however. Of the city's 4400 delinquent vacant lots, about 900 (20 percent) were owned by 63 property-owners who held at least five parcels. Three persons owned 50 or more vacant lots in the city, and 11 persons owned at least 20. Many of these owners purchased their vacant lots for low prices at county forfeiture sales and presumably were not paying taxes pending future disposition of the properties.[e]

Despite the apparent speculation in vacant lots, there was very little tax delinquency in Cleveland among large-scale landlords. This finding confirmed the verbal claims of owners of extensive inner-city holdings of rental properties. As is discussed in Chapter 6, large-scale landlords generally pay their property taxes up until abandonment. Thus Cleveland's tax delinquency problem reflects nonpayment decisions by thousands of single-property owners and a few hundred owners of more than one parcel. Hardly more than 100 people owned over five delinquent properties in 1974.

Survey Implications

The information collected through the survey of delinquent properties in Cleveland has a number of important implications for any revision of the foreclosure process. The major findings may be summarized as follows:

1. The increase in delinquent vacant lots represents a substantial increase in the public's investment in abandoned property. The city of Cleveland spent over $4 million on demolition between 1966 and 1974. The magnitude of this investment heightens the need for alternative forms of compensation for lost revenue.
2. Such investment is likely to continue because eventually the city will demolish many of the unoccupied delinquent buildings that have been vandalized. The high rate of vandalism reduces the already limited value of these properties. It also lessens the feasibility of programs aimed at recycling these properties, such as urban homesteading, by making rehabilitation costs prohibitively high.
3. Over one-half of Cleveland's delinquent parcels contained occupied buildings. Most of these buildings were residential. A change in the foreclosure legislation could therefore affect up to 4.5 percent of the occupied housing units in the city. The marginal or nonexistent profit

---

[e]The figures on multiparcel ownership of delinquent land may slightly understate the case because several different individual or corporate names may be used by groups of investors.

potential of these units would discourage investor interest at tax sales and would also make the local government reluctant to assume responsibility for their management.

4. Delinquent residential structures tend to be small, containing one or two units. The delinquent owners appear to be of two general types: (a) homeowners with low and moderate incomes who are in personal financial difficulty, and (b) small-scale absentee owners who are unwilling to make further investments in wasting assets. Only 12 percent of the 11,100 delinquent parcels in Cleveland are owned by persons responsible for five or more delinquent properties, and nearly 65 percent of their holdings are vacant lots. Thus Cleveland's tax delinquency problem is the result of actions by a large number of individuals, many of whom have been affected by inner-city neighborhood deterioration that was beyond their control.

5. More than half of Cleveland's delinquent, occupied residential structures are owner-occupied. Stricter foreclosure laws could therefore impose hardship upon homeowners with limited incomes, particularly the elderly.

A knowledge of the characteristics of delinquent parcels and their owners assists in anticipation of possible consequences of any revision in the foreclosure process. Chapter 6 provides further description of the fragility of the low-income housing market in the Cleveland neighborhoods where tax delinquency is concentrated.

6

The Fragile Inner-City Housing Market

Our survey of tax delinquent properties in Cleveland revealed that an alarming share of the improved parcels (87 percent) contained *occupied* structures, 88 percent of which were residential buildings. Furthermore, 39 percent of the delinquent occupied residential structures were *owner-occupied*. In other words, approximately 2000 owner-occupied residences and 3100 occupied rental buildings were delinquent in the city of Cleveland. In total, the occupied tax delinquent structures contained a minimum of 10,050 housing units in 1975. Clearly, the policy implications of accelerating the foreclosure process on such properties had to be evaluated thoughtfully. That in turn required analysis of the housing market conditions in central Cleveland where the delinquent parcels were concentrated.

There are three general types of owners of inner-city residential properties: owner-occupants, large-scale landlords, and small- or intermediate-scale landlords. Because each type of owner has distinctly different possessory and operating characteristics, we decided to try to analyze separately the implications of rapid foreclosure for each category of owner. In 1973 the City Planning Commission reviewed low-income housing conditions in Cleveland and found them to be very similar to those of other older, declining central cities.[1] Therefore we hypothesized that we could base our housing demand analysis on survey results from other cities where extensive interview programs had been carried out among inner-city property owners. Rutgers University's Center for Urban Policy Research performed large numbers of in-depth interviews among delinquent and nondelinquent property owners in Newark and New York and among delinquent owners in Pittsburgh.[2] Also, Michael A. Stegman presented partial results of a massive interviewing program in Baltimore in his *Housing Investment in the Inner City;* he focused there on a survey of investors in residential properties.[3]

We recognized that adjustments would have to be made using data from other cities to draw conclusions about Cleveland. Ownership patterns are affected, for example, by differences in construction (such as masonry row houses in Baltimore versus frame single-family homes and duplexes in Cleveland) and by differences in household types (such as

Portions of this chapter appeared in an article by M. Leanne Lachman and J. Denis Gathman in the spring 1976 issue of *Real Estate Review*, and are reprinted with permission.

Pittsburgh's having a disproportionate number of elderly homeowners). There were also differences in the relative decline of the various inner-city neighborhoods when the surveys were undertaken. On a continuum ranging from best to worst, the approximate sequence was Pittsburgh in 1974, Baltimore in 1969, Cleveland in 1975, and Newark in 1971. To verify the hypothesis that we could transfer some of the survey results from other cities to our Cleveland analysis, we performed our own survey of one of the three types of inner-city residential property owners—large-scale landlords. Our findings were remarkably comparable to those of similar surveys in Baltimore, Newark, and New York. Our survey also provided confirming evidence on general inner-city housing market conditions found to exist elsewhere.

Later in this chapter we present the results of our interviews with large-scale residential property owners in central Cleveland, along with our more general conclusions about the other two types of private residential property owners—small-scale landlords and owner-occupants. To place the findings and conclusions of our analysis in perspective, we have first summarized the urban development process in the United States and some of the national and local housing policies that have led to the low-income housing conditions found in central cities generally, and in older, larger cities particularly.

The U.S. Urban Development Process

As Anthony Downs observes, "American urban development occurs in a systematic, highly predictable manner." Furthermore, he argues, "It leads to precisely the results desired by those who dominate it."[4] Most middle- and upper-income urban households enjoy good housing in relatively safe neighborhoods with good public services. In contrast, a high proportion of urban low-income households are concentrated in deteriorating neighborhoods characterized by poorly maintained buildings, overcrowded housing units, high crime, and inappropriate and inadequate social services. Increasingly in older metropolitan areas, the middle- and upper-income households reside in the suburbs, and the moderate- and low-income households remain in the central cities. This is the basic cause of the fiscal crisis of central cities: They contain the majority of the high-cost residents but few of the high-income ones. Tax delinquency is just one symptom/result of this development process.

In the United States and throughout the world, the urban development needed to accommodate population expansion has always occurred predominantly on the edge of the built-up area, where vacant land is available at relatively low cost. Some new construction takes place on vacant parcels that earlier developers skipped over, and some redevelopment of underutilized properties also occurs. However, the vast majority of new construction is on the urban fringe. Each wave of development is planned in accordance with the latest technological and lifestyle changes. Thus each urban ring extending outward from the central or downtown core is more "modern" than the preceding one. This is true of the homes and apartments—which are built in large areas at about the same time—and such community facilities as schools, parks, churches, and shopping centers.

New shacks or minimum-standard structures cannot be built in the United States. Thus low-income households are excluded from new-growth areas. Building and zoning codes require that all new structures be of relatively high quality, so such space is occupied by firms and households that can afford to pay the most. The used buildings vacated by those moving into new space are occupied by companies and households able to pay the next highest prices and rents. Their space is occupied in turn by those at the next level. This descending progression continues until those with the least ability to pay are accommodated in old and obsolete structures. Any left-over buildings are demolished—often after they are abandoned.

This "trickle-down" process of urban development is essentially an economic ladder that matches up quality of space with ability to pay. Because of the legal constraints on new construction, however, the process also correlates income levels with age of structure and, to a large degree, distance from the urban core. As buildings' tenants move downward on the income scale, local authorities tend to become less strict in their enforcement of building codes, which becomes necessary because rehabilitation and maintenance costs would exceed the users' abilities to pay, and legal enforcement of the codes would put the owners out of business and the tenants on the street. When maintenance is deferred, however, buildings deteriorate rapidly.

As housing units trickle down the household income ladder, the neighborhoods in which they are located experience a parallel life cycle. When the housing stock is new, most neighborhoods have a middle- or upper-income character. The neighborhoods tend to reflect currently popular modes of transportation, family and individual lifestyle preferences, and patterns of retailing. As the housing ages, the economic level of the neighborhoods declines, and the land-use patterns gradually become functionally obsolete. Over decades, as the housing trickles down to the lowest income households in the metropolitan area, the neighborhoods deteriorate and become blighted slums.

The record levels of national housing production in 1971, 1972, and 1973 heightened the difficulties in urban ghetto housing markets. New construction, which was largely in the suburbs, far outpaced household formations, and new units were built for an artificial housing market—households leaving central cities for the social amenities of the suburbs. The trickle-down process led to widespread abandonment of units in the most deteriorated neighborhoods of the central cities. Poor households were able to move to better areas, but vacancies remained high even in those areas and prevented rent increases (which low-income tenants could not afford but which would have occurred anyway had demand exceeded supply). Thus abandonment has spread outward geographically in city after city.

As abandonment occurs in the most deteriorated areas and the prior occupants move to adjacent areas, the receiving neighborhoods rapidly decline to levels similar to what was left behind. It can be argued that in the process, poor households actually move into better housing. It is true that dilapidated housing and units without plumbing have largely been eliminated from the urban (but not rural) housing stock since 1960. However, neighborhood blight has spread like a virulent disease. In neighborhood after neighborhood, the psychological environment has become characterized by insecurity as personal violence and property damage have increased. As neighborhoods become places to move out of rather than into, property values fall steadily.

The number of physically sound housing units contaminated by neighborhood blight far exceeds the number of units that have had to be demolished because they were unsafe and unsanitary. In fact, a large proportion of the units that have been abandoned—and subsequently vandalized—were habitable dwellings. It was the neighborhoods that were not considered habitable as soon as the housing market became loose enough to enable residents to leave. This type of neighborhood blight and contamination of structures is still going on and will accelerate as national housing production increases. If we consider environmental deterioration instead of just housing unit deterioration, the housing problem of the poor assumes substantially larger proportions. In fact, what we now see is a two-directional process. New construction causes units to trickle down, whereas abandonment and neighborhood decline promote a "trickle-up" process in which the poor move, in large numbers, into adjacent neighborhoods and trigger property value declines in the receiving areas. This double process has accelerated the pattern of neighborhood change in many central cities.

High vacancies in central cities in the late 1960s and early 1970s have made better housing units available for poor households. At the same time, operating costs have escalated—for labor, fuel, security, and repairs necessitated by vandalism. The incomes of the poor have not risen proportionally, however, so rents have been held down. Therefore market values have fallen and more and more buildings have become unprofitable and have been abandoned by their owners. The economics of public housing projects illustrate the cost squeeze in the low-end real estate market. Because operating costs were escalating but the poverty of tenants prevented necessary rent increases, Congress authorized operating subsidies for public housing units as early as 1969 and 1970. Local housing authorities have claimed that the approved subsidies are inadequate because of further cost/revenue disparities. Operating costs in Cleveland's public housing projects rose by 70 percent in the four-year period from 1970 to 1974. Administrative costs went up 90 percent, utilities increased 80 percent, and insurance premiums rose 111 percent.[5] Similar financial problems have been encountered in the private low-income housing market, and the results have been tax delinquency and abandonment.

Survey of Large-Scale Landlords

To determine how changes in the Cuyahoga County foreclosure process would affect inner-city landlords controlling large numbers of properties, and to verify the similarity between Cleveland's low-income housing conditions and those of Baltimore, Newark, and Pittsburgh, Real Estate Research Corporation staff members conducted one- to two-hour interviews with a dozen of the largest owners and operators of rental housing for the poor. Ten of the interviewees were owners of ghetto properties and two were lawyers representing landlords. Together, these people owned 1400 rental units and 600 vacant lots, and they managed another 520 rental units. Almost all the properties were in Hough and Glenville—two of the most deteriorated areas on Cleveland's East Side. The 1920 units rented by these landlords represented approximately 4 percent of the total housing units in the area, and roughly 4.5 percent of the privately owned units. (There were 5643 public housing units in central East Side neighborhoods of Cleveland in mid-1975).

Persons to be interviewed in the landlord survey were selected from the recorded and known owners and managers of twenty-five or more residential structures on the city's East Side. Although the basic list used for the sample was comprehensive, it was not definitive because recorded deeds can be in many different individual and corporate names. However, we verified the list with persons interviewed and found it to be reasonably complete. Interestingly, only twenty-five names appeared on the list, and there was some duplication because relatives investing together were listed separately. This small number of large-scale landlords accords with findings in Newark and Baltimore. George Sternlieb and Robert W. Burchell found in 1972 that only 1.6 percent of the 313 properties in their

Newark sample were held by persons who owned over 75 housing units, and just 10.5 percent of the owners in the sample had more than 13 units.[6] In Baltimore in the late 1960s, Stegman reports that "over one-fourth of the private inner-city rental inventory is owned or controlled by about 50 professionals, with the largest having in excess of 1500 units and the smallest, about 100."[7] He estimates that medium-sized investors with between 25 and 100 units controlled 15 percent of the rental units, and the remaining 60 percent were in the hands of small and casual investors with less than 25 units.

In Cleveland in 1975, there were neither as many large landlords as Stegman found in Baltimore, nor as many properties controlled by such owners. One owner in our survey had only 5 rental units, but the majority managed over 100 housing units. The most extensive holdings were 500 units owned by one man and 400 units owned and/or managed by each of two others. Two of the people interviewed also owned several hundred vacant lots, most of which were purchased at forfeiture sales. One-half of the owners focused primarily on large apartment buildings. The remainder, including one of the 400-unit managers, rented out houses and two- and four-flat buildings.

Most of the nearly 2000 housing units controlled by the twelve persons interviewed were located in deteriorated neighborhoods of Cleveland. Thus these landlords were major suppliers of private market housing for the poor in mid-1975. The findings and inferences cited below from Real Estate Research Corporation's survey reveal the precarious balance that existed between solvency and insolvency in Cleveland's ghetto housing market. The trend was definitely toward red ink on the balance sheet.

Characteristics of Cleveland's Large-Scale Owners

All ten owners interviewed had been investing in rental housing in Cleveland for twelve years or more. The median number of years of real estate ownership was twenty-seven, and the average was twenty-eight years. Eight of the ten owners were white, and all were male. Many of the currently held buildings had been owned by the interviewees from the time they were rented to middle-income whites. Subsequently, tenancy consisted of middle- and moderate-income blacks. By 1975 virtually 100 percent of the tenants were low-income blacks. Because of the length of ownership, most of the structures did not carry mortgages, a characteristic that Stegman also found in the properties of the more than thirty large-scale owners interviewed in Baltimore. Based on other survey data from the late sixties in Baltimore, Stegman observes, "Almost 30 percent of the units in the inner city are mortgaged, with the majority of the encumbered structures being held by nonlarge investors. Because of the mortgage payments, these units cannot possibly throw off any cash."[8]

Rent Levels of Owned /Managed Housing

The rents obtained in inner-city structures by the landlords interviewed reflect the poverty of the tenants. The ranges of reported rents for unfurnished apartments in June 1975 (including utilities) were as follows:

Size of unit	Monthly rent range
3 rooms	$60–$85
4 rooms	$60–$90
5 rooms	$55–$100
6 rooms	$75–$130

The ratio of rent to income that is considered "normal" in the United States is 25 percent, but the usual proportion for the poor is at least 35 percent. Using both these ratios, we have calculated the probable annual incomes of tenants at various reported rental levels. For example:

Monthly rent	Annual income if rent were 25%	Annual income if rent were 35%
$60	$2880	$2060
$85	$4080	$2910
$130	$6240	$4460

These suggested income levels match the 1970 Census figures for the neighborhoods of the units. In Hough, the median income for families and unrelated individuals was about $3500. In Glenville, the median was $6245, but it declined significantly after 1970. To put these incomes in perspective, one person working full time for forty hours a week at a minimum hourly wage of $2.10 would earn $4368 per year. As another comparison, the upper income limits for Cleveland public housing units ranged in 1972 from $3600 for a one-person household to $7000 for a ten-member household. Rents for individual qualifying households had a maximum limit of 23 percent of income. Thus the landlords surveyed by RERC draw their tenants from the same income groups as the public housing agency. Some of the landlords complained, in fact, that the housing authority accepted the better tenants and did not admit the households with the most serious problems.

Three of the landlords did not rent to welfare recipients. The other people interviewed said that the proportions of their tenants on welfare ranged from a low of 10 percent to a high of 75 percent; the average was 50 percent. Rents were collected monthly, and tenants were generally fifteen to thirty days behind in rent payments. The reported collection losses were from 5 percent to 20 percent; however, a substantial additional cost was incurred when tenants were evicted. When repairs, redecoration, legal fees, and rent losses were totaled, eviction reportedly cost landlords between $400 and $600 per unit.[a] These figures are higher than those estimated by Stegman in 1969 for Baltimore row houses. In comparison to normal turnover, which he felt could easily cost $200 per unit, Stegman calculated that eviction losses averaged about $300 per unit, considering foregone back rent, redecoration, and rent losses between tenants.[9] Part of the difference between the two cities may be accounted for by Baltimore's relatively smoothly operating housing court, where evictions are handled expeditiously. In comparison to cash flows, Stegman found that turnover and eviction costs were substantial for the single-family row houses that predominate in Baltimore's inner-city housing inventory. He says, "Turnover costs, including lost rent and redecorating expenses, can easily total about two years' cash flow, while it costs about five years' cash flow to repair a badly vandalized unit."[10]

Income and Expenses for Low-Income Rental Housing

Table 6–1 shows a typical operating pro forma for a Cleveland apartment building in Hough or Glenville in mid-1975. The data in the pro forma reflect information supplied by landlords we interviewed and our general knowledge of low-income housing markets. For comparison, we have also shown typical operating ratios for an older middle-income apartment building of the same size. The key conclusion is the bottom line. Net operating income for the low-income building (before financing costs and income taxes) is estimated to be 20 percent of gross, which compares very unfavorably with the 38-percent figure for the middle-income building. Other findings demonstrated by this comparison are:

1. One of the most serious factors inhibiting profitable operation of low-income buildings is the high loss from vacancy and noncollection of rent. We used a 15 percent figure for this (as compared to 5 percent, which is a relatively high figure, for a normal older apartment building), though some of the landlords we interviewed said that their loss was significantly greater than 15 percent. Generally, the large-scale landlords had a lower vacancy rate than the surrounding

[a] Visits to the housing court by Cleveland City Planning Commission staff in fall 1975 indicated that eviction costs were indeed substantial.

Table 6–1
1975 Pro Forma Operating Statements for Older Low- and Middle-Income Apartment Buildings in Cleveland

	Typical Cleveland Low-Income Building	*Typical Cleveland Middle-Income Building*
Gross annual income	100%	100%
Less vacancy and collection loss	15	5
Effective gross annual income	85%	95%
Operating expenses:		
Decorating	4	5
Advertising and promotion	1	2
General supplies and maintenance	3	1
Operating payroll	10	8
Payroll taxes	1	1
Management	6	5
Water and sewer	2	1
Property insurance	3	2
Real estate taxes	18	16
Services	1	1
Heat	10	9
Electric	4	3
Miscellaneous	2	3
Total operating expenses	65%	57%
Net operating income	20%	38%

Source: Real Estate Research Corporation estimates.

neighborhood. In Hough and Glenville, vacancy in rental units was perceived as being as high as 20 percent in early summer 1975, whereas most of the owners in our survey said their vacancies were between 7 percent and 10 percent, having risen three to seven percentage points since their original purchases of the buildings. Collection losses were added to the vacancy before arriving at effective gross income. The owners said that rent collection was a more serious problem than vacancy rates.

2. Utility costs have risen rapidly for apartment buildings across the country, but particularly in the Northeast. The U.S. Department of Labor estimated that electricity costs in Cleveland rose 29 percent in 1974; there were further increases in 1975. In many housing markets, tenants pay utilities, so landlords have to absorb the costs only for lighting and heating common areas. In inner-city Cleveland, however, landlords pay all utilities, which has proven exceptionally hard on owners of buildings with low-income tenants because it has been impossible to pass so large a cost increase on to the renters.

3. With the exception of one manager of an FHA-financed apartment

building and one other owner, none of the landlords had mortgages on their apartments. That is why buildings with such high operating expenses could still be held by private owners. Nonetheless, one-half the landlords interviewed said they would need 25 percent rent increases to make their properties good investments. All said that rents could not be raised that much. These observations confirm Stegman's comment about Baltimore: "If taxes were lowered or if some other costs were brought into line, the benefits would not be passed on to the tenant. Instead, they would be absorbed by investors until an acceptable profit picture emerged, at which time an upward recapitalization of values could be expected."[11] This situation has also been revealed in some of the housing allowance experiments conducted for the U.S. Department of Housing and Urban Development. Structural improvement of units rented by housing allowance recipients has not been nearly as extensive as originally envisioned, undoubtedly because many landlords needed the allowances to bring their basic returns to acceptable levels.

4. The rates of return reported by the Cleveland landlords were slightly lower than those found in Baltimore in 1969 and in Newark in 1971. In all three cities, though, there was enormous variation among owners. In no cases were the general returns high in relation to the original purchase prices of the buildings and the improbability of future capital gains. Stegman concluded in Baltimore that "With a few notable exceptions, investors who are earning a great deal of money do so by obtaining modest cash flow on many hundreds of unencumbered units, rather than through high yields."[12]

Key Management Problems Cited by Landlords

The questionnaire used in Cleveland was open-ended, so the property owners and managers were not asked to rank their perceived difficulties in order of seriousness. Nor were they provided with a full list of potential problems to comment upon. Nonetheless, their major concerns became apparent as they answered specific questions about tenant relations, real estate assessment, building inspection, crime, rent collection, etc. The key problems inhibiting maintenance and reinvestment are shown in Table 6–2. For comparison, Sternlieb and Burchell's more systematic findings regarding all types of Newark ghetto owners in 1971 are also shown.

As may be seen, the order of priority of problems was quite different in Newark and Cleveland. This partially reflects the changes that occurred throughout the Northeast in the four years between 1971 and 1975

Table 6–2

Relative Importance of Operating Problems of Inner-City Landlords in Cleveland and Newark

(listed in order of significance)

Cleveland—1975	Newark—1971
Tenants	Tax level
Neighborhood problems	Neighborhood problems
Energy cost increases	Tenants
Building inspection problems	Building inspection problems
Tax level	Mortgage cost
Hazard insurance	Hazard insurance

Source: Real Estate Research Corporation interviews with large-scale Cleveland landlords, and George Sternlieb and Robert W. Burchell, *Residential Abandonment: The Tenement Landlord Revisited* (New Brunswick, N.J.: Center for Urban Policy Research, 1973), p. 115. The Newark study covered all types of property owners; large-scale landlords were a small proportion of the total sample.

(especially skyrocketing energy costs). However, it is significant that taxes were not considered the burden in Cleveland that they were in Newark. Landlords felt that Cleveland's tax court was fair. Their income statements were taken into account, and they generally viewed the taxes as reasonable. (As will be discussed later, the landlords for the most part were paying the property taxes on all their buildings.) Had we interviewed owners of single properties, who might not have known of the appeals process, taxes might have ranked higher on the list of key problems. However, staff members of Squire, Sanders & Dempsey, the law firm that participated in this study, examined the tax appeals process and concluded that it was not too complex for the average property owner to execute without a lawyer.

Tenant relations, the key problem for large-scale landlords in Cleveland, will be discussed in the next section. Neighborhood problems and energy cost increases have already been covered. Building inspection was perceived as an unnecessary irritant by most of the landlords. Only three of the twelve people interviewed believed that code inspections were conducted properly. Most of the interviewees complained that inspection standards were too high, mentioning examples of citations received for trash on lawns and for furniture piled in a corner of a basement. The owners did not feel, in light of their other difficulties, that these were maintenance defects worthy of citation.

All respondents said that they had had housing code violations at one time or another. Only one owner said that he had demolished buildings rather than bring them up to code.

Landlord/Tenant Relations

Increases in energy costs were foremost in landlords' minds because they were direct—and also unexpected—expenses at the time of the Cleveland survey, but the primary long-term concern was the behavior of tenants. Although many low-income tenants took care of their apartments and paid their rents promptly, more and more were described as being "problem" occupants who damaged property, disturbed their neighbors, and were chronically late with rent payments. Crime and vandalism levels were very high, and landlords found it difficult to hire custodians and property managers for their buildings.

A new constraint on inner-city landlords in Ohio is the Landlord-Tenant Bill (S.B.) 103, which became effective on November 4, 1974. All the landlords visited for the survey were aware of the legislation and were concerned about it, though it had not been in effect long enough for its impact to be felt. The bill includes numerous safeguards and prohibitions on both landlords and tenants, though the emphasis is on redressing the historic onesidedness of the rental situation wherein the landlord has always been right and in control.

Unless housing inspectors and judges use discretion in interpreting the bill, the legislation could be considered to be excessively restrictive when applied to low-rent housing units. The tenants of low-rent housing often are not financially capable of paying rents that would enable the owner to maintain the property in standard condition. Like acceleration of the foreclosure process, the landlord–tenant bill may have unintended consequences—such as increased abandonment. Any government intervention in the low-income housing market must be considered carefully. There is a need to strike a balance between the tenants' need for recourse against landlords who do not provide basic housing requirements and the economic realities faced by the owners of inner-city residential properties.

Perceptions of Future Worth of Buildings

With the exception of two persons who thought that the limited supply of remaining housing units might cause an increase in the value of their structures, all the white landlords interviewed in Real Estate Research Corporation's survey felt that their properties in central Cleveland would be worth less in five years. The two black landlords were more optimistic and observed that residual owners were starting to improve their properties. These two men also thought that they could recapture investments in structural improvements if they sold their buildings. The whites did not believe such recapture was possible.

Three of the owners had made substantial improvements in their properties over the prior five years (kitchens, floors, gutters, and so forth). Eight of the ten building owners reported replacing boilers since 1970. Otherwise no major improvements had been made, and three landlords said they made no investments at all. All owners said that they would not be able to obtain mortgages on their properties if they were to try, but two people had financed building improvements with personal bank loans.

Tax Delinquency Among Large-Scale Owners

Except for an FHA-owned property managed by one person interviewed and two persons who refused to answer, all the landlords said they did not have tax delinquent structures. Three people reported that they had vacant lots on which they were not paying taxes because they felt the lots had no value.[b] The consensus among the owners was that they would abandon buildings when revenues from those buildings would not cover taxes. In other words, they would stop paying taxes and abandon their properties simultaneously. None of the landlords would comment on how long they intended to keep their properties operating.

The finding in Cleveland that most large-scale rental property owners in the inner city did not have tax delinquent structures is consistent with survey results in other cities. In his analysis of rent-controlled properties in New York in the late 1960s, George Sternlieb found, for example, that "It is the structures which are in the largest and strongest hands which are least delinquent. The older, smaller buildings in the sample, those with typically less sophisticated owners, reveal the highest delinquency rate."[13] More specifically, he states, "Owners of under seven parcels comprise two-thirds of the delinquents. This is somewhat less than the equivalent for non-delinquents. On the other hand, the largest scale operators, those with over 12 parcels, are under represented among the delinquents."[14] The parcels Sternlieb refers to are multiunit New York City apartment buildings, so fewer structures are needed to qualify an owner as large-scale. Sternlieb's findings in Newark and Stegman's in Baltimore also support the thesis that owners of large numbers of unencumbered units who have their own management and maintenance staffs have greater staying power than small-scale landlords in inner-city declining housing markets.

---

[b] The landlords' comments on their own tax delinquency were subsequently verified by checking print-outs of the names of property owners with five or more delinquent properties. The large-scale landlords in the survey showed up on the list for vacant land but not on that for improved properties.

When asked what the effects would be if the foreclosure process were accelerated in Cleveland, the landlords' responses were equally divided among improvement, no change, and worsening of real estate conditions in the inner city. Those who said foreclosure should be accelerated were the landlords who tended to answer other questions optimistically. No one felt there would be a market for foreclosed improved parcels, but some mentioned that vacant lots could be purchased for more realistic prices at sheriff's sales. Those who believed that accelerated foreclosure would not make a difference in the area expressed the opinion that owners were ready to abandon their properties anyway. The remaining group of owners felt that abandonment would rise—one owner said it would double—if foreclosure were accelerated. All the landlords felt that abandonment in the inner city would continue at high levels no matter what was done about the speed of foreclosure.

Cleveland's Tax Delinquent Property-Owners

We do not know enough in Cleveland or in other cities, with the possible exception of Pittsburgh, to prepare a definitive profile of tax delinquent property-owners. However, we can make some reasonable assumptions and draw preliminary conclusions on the basis of the information that is now available on tax delinquency and low-income, inner-city housing markets.

For our analysis, we divided owners of delinquent residential properties into three categories, as follows:

1. Owner-occupants—Based on the City Planning Commission's review of over one-half the delinquent parcels in Cleveland, approximately 2000 residential structures with unpaid back taxes were occupied by their owners in mid-1975. Of these structures, about 1300 were single-family homes, 600 were duplexes, and 100 were multifamily buildings with three or more units.
2. Small-scale landlords—The majority of the 3100 renter-occupied delinquent buildings in Cleveland were owned by persons with less than five delinquent structures. Although these landlords might have owned many other nondelinquent buildings, it is unlikely that a large number of them had widespread real estate holdings. Such a pattern would not be consistent with findings in other cities. Nor would it mesh with the tax behavior of the large-scale landlords interviewed by Real Estate Research Corporation. We estimate that 2800 of the 3100 delinquent renter-occupied buildings were owned by so-called small-scale landlords.

3. Larger-scale landlords—Only 51 property owners in Cleveland had five or more delinquent improved properties in 1974. Although ownership of five properties hardly qualifies as "large scale" in real estate circles, it was the final cutoff point in the Cleveland delinquency data that still left a meaningful number of properties in the last category. A total of 480 properties were owned by these persons, of which an estimated 300 were occupied residential structures and the remainder were vacant buildings or nonresidential structures.

As shown in Table 6–3, we allocated delinquent housing units in Cleveland among the three types of landlords by size of structure. The distribution of owner-occupied units is based on survey findings, but the allocations of units between small- and larger-scale owners are our own estimates. According to this distribution, 3000 housing units were in buildings occupied by the owner; 5800 units were in buildings owned by small-scale landlords; and 1200 housing units were rented by larger-scale landlords.

In evaluating residential delinquency in Cleveland, we attempted to distinguish what might be called "normal" tax delinquency from "problem" delinquency. By "normal," we meant short-term delinquencies caused primarily by temporary financial difficulties of either homeowners or landlords. As an approximation of those units, we removed from our analysis the 2700 housing units in delinquent residential structures located in Stage 1 and 1.5 neighborhoods. Generally, those are the areas in Cleveland with rising real estate values and active resale markets. Thus

Table 6–3
Estimated Distribution of Cleveland's Delinquent Housing Units Among Key Types of Property-Owners

Type of Owner	*Total Structures*[a]	*Single-Family Units*	*Units in Duplexes*	*Units in Multi-family Buildings*	*Estimated Total Units*
Owner-occupants[a]	2,000	1,300	1,200	500	3,000
Small-scale landlords (under 5 delinquent structures)	2,800	1,200	2,100	2,500	5,800
Larger-scale landlords (5 or more delinquent structures)	300	—	300	900	1,200
Total[a]	5,100	2,500	3,600	3,900	10,000

Source: Real Estate Research Corporation estimates.
[a]Based on Cleveland City Planning Commission's 1975 field survey.

they are areas where redemption of delinquent properties would be likely and where foreclosure sale prices would be relatively high.[c] The field inspections in those areas did not indicate that the delinquent structures were blighting influences on their surrounding areas. Among the occupied residential structures that were delinquent in Stage 1 areas, only 7.5 percent were in worse condition than adjacent buildings; and the comparable figure in Stage 1.5 neighborhoods was 9.3 percent. Given these findings, there did not seem to be special reasons to accelerate the foreclosure process in Cleveland's stable or nearly stable residential areas.

To provide an estimate of "problem" residential tax delinquency, we removed the units in Stage 1 and 1.5 areas from the totals in Table 6–3. Table 6–4 sets forth the estimated distribution of delinquent housing units in Cleveland's declining neighborhoods by type of owner. Nearly three-quarters of the housing units in delinquent structures in the city are located in Stage 2 to 4.5 areas where low- and moderate-income households predominate. As indicated in Table 6–4, an estimated 22 percent of the delinquent units in these areas are in owner-occupied buildings, 62 percent are in buildings owned by small-scale landlords, and 16 percent are rented by larger-scale landlords. Half the units are in buildings with three or more units, one-third are in duplexes, and one-sixth are single-family homes.

Earlier we described the characteristics of larger-scale Cleveland landlords. Although most of the property owners and managers we interviewed did not have tax delinquent structures and were probably better capitalized than their delinquent counterparts, their operating experience and their problems in renting to low-income tenants are typical. General profiles of the other two categories of delinquent inner-city property owners—owner-occupants and small-scale landlords—can be developed from the surveys conducted in Pittsburgh, Newark, and, to a lesser extent, Baltimore. After making some adjustments for structural differences in the Cleveland housing inventory and after removing from consideration the delinquent units in stable residential areas, we believe that the following profiles of delinquent homeowners and small-scale landlords are sufficiently representative for policy analyses.[d] The general characteristics of delinquent homeowners are:

[c] In the Pittsburgh study, Sternlieb et al. found that owners who perceived that their properties were increasing in value tended to have lower rates and absolute amounts of delinquency—and maintained their buildings better—than owners who perceived that their properties were decreasing in value (*The Magnitude and Determinants of Property Tax Delinquency in Pittsburgh*, II, p. 105).

[d] The profiles of delinquent owners draw heavily on Sternlieb et al.'s Pittsburgh study, as well as Sternlieb's surveys in Newark, though specific characteristics have been added or modified in accordance with findings from the Cleveland survey of tax delinquent properties and other work by the Cleveland City Planning Commission.

Table 6–4
Approximate Ownership Pattern of Lower-Income Delinquent Housing Units in Cleveland in 1975

Type of Owner	Single-Family Units	Units in Duplexes	Units in Multi-Family Buildings	Total Units
Owner-occupants	600	600	400	1,600
Small-scale landlords (under 5 delinquent structures)	600	1,500	2,400	4,500
Larger-scale landlords (5 or more delinquent structures)	—	300	900	1,200
Total	1,200	2,400	3,700	7,300

Source: Real Estate Research Corporation estimates.

Note: Excludes delinquent housing units in Stage 1 and 1.5 areas. Only units in Stage 2 through 4.5 areas are included.

1. Their annual incomes are under $10,000 and frequently under $5000.
2. Usually they have lived in their units for over ten years and often for over twenty-five years; thus many are older persons.
3. Most have no other real estate holdings.
4. Their occupations vary from laborers to professionals, but up to 25 percent depend on fixed incomes.
5. They tend to be more positive about the future of their neighborhoods than are rental property owners, except when racial transition is underway.
6. They expect to make tax payments eventually.

The general characteristics of small-scale delinquent landlords are:

1. Their annual incomes are frequently under $10,000.
2. The owners are often white, and their properties are usually in predominantly black areas.
3. They own a small number of marginal properties, often just one building.
4. They are frequently pessimistic about the future of the neighborhoods.
5. Between one-third and one-half do not intend to pay further taxes.
6. They often inherited the delinquent properties.

For many of these delinquent property-owners in declining areas, back taxes represent a high proportion of their properties' market values, or even exceed them. Thus full payment is unlikely—both because the owners do not have the money and because redemption is not an economically sound option. Yet most of the properties are not marketable at foreclosure sales either, because they cannot be operated profitably. Thus local governments are in a bind: They are losing taxes but they will not benefit from foreclosure. In fact, they run the risk of ending up in control of substandard residential buildings that have been abandoned by their owners and are either legally or illegally occupied. In inner-city areas, tax delinquency is usually a precursor or corollary of abandonment. Furthermore, taxes do not appear to be a key cause of the abandonment. Neighborhood decay, crime, destructive tenants, and soaring utility costs are much more serious problems for property-owners than taxes.

Essentially, therefore, tax delinquency in inner-city areas is a function of low-income housing economics. Owners of most residential units rented to low-income tenants need more income before they can even provide adequate maintenance. Many small-scale owners—and more and more larger ones—are earning no return on their investments because vacancies are too high in the inner-city to permit rent increases and the tenants cannot afford higher rents anyway.[e] Caught between rising operating costs and static or declining rent rolls, property-owners are abandoning their buildings and/or allowing them to become tax delinquent. Rapid or concerted foreclosure will not force the owners of low-rent apartments to "pay up," nor will it enable the public to acquire income-producing, marketable properties. Furthermore, the owner-occupied delinquent structures would be no more marketable than the rental buildings if acquired through foreclosure, and displacement of the owners would remove a stabilizing element that is badly needed in declining neighborhoods.

Our analyses of the economics of low-income housing markets and the characteristics of tax delinquent property owners led us to the conclusion that foreclosure should not be accelerated for improved properties. We believe that a rapid foreclosure process would cause an increase in abandonment and eventual acquisition by the local government of legally occupied buildings abandoned by the owners. Thus the city would assume

---

[e] If the collapse of private low-income housing markets becomes more severe and demolition catches up with abandonment, supply and demand may become more evenly matched. Then structures abandoned by their owners will still be occupied because there will not be vacant units available for the tenants to move into. In the short run, overcrowding will intensify as poor households double up to pay higher rents, and there will be an increase in the squatter population, which is already large in many older cities. In the longer run, there are only two alternatives: (1) tremendous housing subsidies will have to be created to cover the gap between the cost of operating housing for the poor and the rent that tenants can afford; or (2) local governments will by default become the landlords of the poor. In the latter instance, if the cost/income gap is not covered somehow, local governments will have to reconcile themselves to operating units at quality standards that are now illegal.

the high costs and very considerable problems of being housers of last resort.

Notes

1. Cleveland City Planning Commission, *Cleveland Housing Papers*, March 1973.

2. George Sternlieb and Robert W. Burchell, *Residential Abandonment: The Tenement Landlord Revisited* (New Brunswick, N. J.: Center for Urban Policy Research, 1973); George Sternlieb, *The Urban Housing Dilemma: The Dynamics of New York City's Rent Controlled Housing* (New York: Housing and Development Administration, 1972); George Sternlieb, Robert W. Lake, and Franklin J. James, *The Magnitude and Determinants of Property Tax Delinquency in Pittsburgh*, volume II: "Survey Analysis and Recommendations" (New Brunswick, N. J.: Center for Urban Policy Research, 1974).

3. Michael Stegman, *Housing Investment in the Inner City: The Dynamics of Decline* (Cambridge, Mass.: MIT Press, 1972).

4. Anthony Downs, *Opening Up the Suburbs: An Urban Strategy for America* (New Haven, Conn.: Yale University Press, 1973), p. 1. This section of the chapter draws heavily upon Anthony Downs's writing and analyses.

5. Cuyahoga Metropolitan Housing Authority, *Annual Reports*, 1970–1974.

6. Sternlieb and Burchell, *Residential Abandonment*, p. 60.

7. Stegman, *Housing Investment in the Inner City*, p. 27.

8. Ibid., p. 45.

9. Ibid.

10. Ibid., p. 91.

11. Ibid.

12. Ibid., p. 90.

13. Sternlieb, *The Urban Housing Dilemma*, p. 418.

14. Ibid., p. 424.

Conclusions and Recommendations

Our analysis revealed that real property tax delinquency is likely to remain a serious problem in the city of Cleveland in the coming years. In 1974 the owners of more than 11,000 parcels, or 6.5 percent of all parcels in the city, had failed to pay outstanding taxes or special assessments. Delinquent taxes on real property, excluding public utility property, totaled $12.6 million. The number of delinquent parcels has grown at an increasing rate: three times as many parcels became delinquent between 1970 and 1974 as in the previous four years. If this continues, almost 18,000 parcels will be delinquent in Cleveland by 1978. Although almost one-half of the delinquent parcels are located in the city's six most deteriorated neighborhoods, the problem has begun to spread into areas that are only in initial stages of decline.

Existing tax foreclosure procedures have proved inadequate to deal with the scope of Cleveland's delinquency problem. The current foreclosure process is both time consuming and costly, and the vast increase in the number of delinquent parcels has rendered it virtually inoperative. The current law allows foreclosure after a property has been delinquent for approximately two years, but it has taken an average of ten years for properties to be offered at tax sales. Only a small portion of the eligible parcels are actually offered at the tax sales, largely because of the cost of the foreclosure procedure.

There appears to be little interest in the purchase of property at tax sales. Many parcels remain unsold, and those that sell are purchased for low prices. Not only has the process failed to recover a significant portion of the delinquent taxes, but the county has also spent thousands of dollars in administrative costs bringing these parcels to the point of foreclosure. Often the administrative costs are not recovered through the sales procedure either. Finally, many of those who purchase parcels at tax sales fail to pay taxes on their new acquisitions. Half the Cleveland parcels sold at tax sales in a recent six-year period became delinquent again within three years after the sale. Many of these parcels will move through the costly foreclosure process again, adding to the public's investment, and reinvestment, in them.

Clearly, Ohio's property tax foreclosure process needed revision. During our research into the delinquency problem, however, it became apparent that any proposed solutions would have to recognize the fact that tax delinquency is a symptom of the problems inherent in declining

129

inner-city areas. Revision of the foreclosure statute would have to consider the economic realities of the inner-city land market if it were to:

1. Avoid imposing undue hardship on low-income property owners and tenants.
2. Reduce expenditures for administrative costs on property in which the public already has a substantial investment.

Our research indicated a number of factors that have contributed to the difficulties currently experienced by those who administer the existing foreclosure procedure and, in addition, by the owners of delinquent parcels. Property is becoming delinquent as a result of circumstances that have caused the value of land in entire neighborhoods of the city to decline. Among the research findings that created a framework for our analysis of the foreclosure process were the following:

1. *Tax delinquency is directly correlated with the process of neighborhood decline.* Almost 70 percent of Cleveland's delinquent parcels at the end of 1974 were located in declining neighborhoods. Over half the parcels were in areas that could be classified as being in advanced stages of decline. In West Hough, one of the most deteriorated areas of the city, 32 percent of the parcels were tax delinquent in December 1974. This compares to a citywide figure of 6.5 percent and delinquency rates of 1.5 percent to 3.0 percent in stable residential neighborhoods.
2. *Most tenants of tax delinquent residential properties in declining areas have low incomes.* Their incomes have not been increasing at rates anywhere near those of housing operating costs. Consequently, landlords have not been able to raise rents enough to cover their costs, and tax delinquency has become a frequent precursor to abandonment.
3. *Nearly 40 percent of the occupied residential structures that were tax delinquent in December 1974 were the primary homes of their owners.* Many of the owner-occupied residences with delinquent taxes were in healthy neighborhoods and in most cases were short-term delinquencies caused by temporary financial problems. We estimate, however, that between one-fifth and one-fourth of the delinquent occupied residential buildings in declining neighborhoods were owner-occupied. Those owners tend to have low incomes and little equity apart from their investments in the buildings they live in. Their low incomes have made property taxes a financial burden.
4. *As the population drops in declining areas, vacancy rates increase.* There has been substantial outmigration from inner-city areas in

Cleveland, and the corresponding increases in the vacancy rates have made property ownership less profitable.

5. *As a result of the preceding factors, the market values of the vast majority of delinquent parcels have been steadily declining.* In parts of West Hough and West Central, properties containing vandalized structures actually have a negative value because the land is worth less than the cost of demolition. The declining values of tax delinquent parcels are reflected in the low prices obtained at foreclosure sales.

6. *It appears that the tax delinquency problem is the result of the decisions of a large number of property owners, rather than that of a few large-scale owners.* Only fifty-one owners had five or more delinquent improved properties. Approximately 80 percent of the city's 4100 delinquent vacant lots were owned by individuals or corporations who held fewer than five delinquent parcels.

When inner-city tax delinquency is evaluated in the context of the low-income housing market, where property values are declining and buildings are actually being abandoned by their owners, it is not realistic to adopt a hard-line foreclosure policy. In many cases owners would abandon their properties rather than continue to invest money in them by paying taxes. This abandonment would impose hardship on low-income residents who are displaced, and it would increase the city's responsibilities for demolition of condemned structures.

We therefore recommended revisions in the foreclosure process that would reduce the administrative expenses associated with foreclosure and provide a means of compensation for government investment in abandoned property, while recognizing the fragile nature of the low-income housing market. In our analysis, the following questions emerged as the primary issues to be resolved:

1. How can administrative costs of foreclosure be decreased, and efficiency increased, while still protecting the rights of property-owners?
2. How can the city and other taxing districts be compensated for lost tax revenues and property maintenance expenditures?
3. Should a municipal land reutilization program acquire occupied, residential properties?
4. How can any hardships imposed on residential property owners as a result of foreclosure be minimized?

On the basis of the analysis performed by the Cleveland City Planning Commission and Real Estate Research Corporation staff on these issues, the law firm of Squire, Sanders & Dempsey drafted a bill that was introduced in the Ohio State Legislature in spring 1976. After minor revisions, the law was passed and was signed by the governor. A summary of the legislation, prepared by the Cleveland City Planning Commission, is included in Appendix B.

Each of the four primary issues behind the legislation is discussed in turn on the following pages. The research findings that were considered in arriving at our recommendations are summarized. At the end of the discussion of each issue, we have briefly stated the recommendations that were incorporated in the legislation.

Issue 1: How Can Administrative Costs of Tax Foreclosure Be Decreased, and Efficiency Increased, While Still Protecting the Rights of Property-Owners?

Ohio law allows the prosecutor to begin foreclosure one year after a parcel has been certified delinquent, which would be approximately two years after tax payments were first missed. The foreclosure process previously involved notification of all persons who had any interest in a delinquent property. These individuals were identified by a title search and were notified according to the rules of civil procedure. Before a property was offered for sale, three separate appraisals were also obtained. The delinquent parcels were then offered at a tax sale for two-thirds of their appraised values, and if not sold were reoffered at subsequent sales. The court could order additional appraisals and could reduce the minimum allowable bid. Any parcels that were not sold at the second or third sales were forfeited to the state, and the county auditor then offered them to the highest bidder at a forfeiture sale.

The rising volume of delinquent parcels in the city of Cleveland slowed this process down considerably. In 1974 there were over 11,000 delinquent parcels, an increase of 37 percent since 1966. Most of this increase occurred between 1970 and 1974, when almost 2300 parcels became delinquent. Approximately one-half of the parcels had been delinquent long enough to be eligible for the initiation of foreclosure proceedings, but the magnitude of the problem placed a heavy burden on the county officials responsible for foreclosure. Because of budgetary limitations, only a small portion of the eligible parcels were actually offered at tax sales—less than 230 parcels in 1973 and 1974. It has taken approximately ten years after a parcel has been certified delinquent before it has actually been offered at a tax sale.

The cost of the historic procedure added significantly to the public's investment in delinquent property. Quantifiable administrative costs incurred in bringing a delinquent parcel to sale averaged approximately $400. These costs do not include staff time spent compiling delinquent land lists, preparing and checking advertisements, notifying owners, organizing sales, and so forth.

The amounts expended for administrative costs seem particularly significant in light of the results of the foreclosure sales. Just over one-third of the parcels offered at the sheriff's sales in 1969 to 1971 were sold, and only 23 percent of the parcels offered in 1973 and 1974 were sold. Approximately 28 percent of the parcels disposed of at sheriff's sales in 1969 to 1971, and almost 20 percent of the parcels sold in 1973 and 1974, were purchased for less than $500. The auditor's sales of forfeited land have had higher rates of sale, but the purchase prices have been much lower. Although over 80 percent of the parcels offered by the auditor in 1969 and 1972 were sold, only 5 percent were purchased for over $500 and one-third sold for $50 or less. The purchase prices at forfeiture sales rarely allow for even the recovery of administrative costs, let alone back taxes.

Clearly, the costs incurred in foreclosing upon delinquent parcels frequently do not reflect the low values of the properties being processed. The lack of bidders for delinquent properties often necessitates the reoffering of parcels at subsequent sales, resulting in additional administrative expenditures. It appears that the number of tax delinquent parcels in Cleveland will continue to increase. Therefore the workload and administrative costs of foreclosure will also rise. Any administrative changes that streamline the process, while still protecting the rights of property-owners, will reduce the expenses being charged to taxing districts.

Recommendations on Issue 1

A number of recommended administrative changes were included in the bill introduced into the Ohio State Legislature in the spring of 1976. Key among them were the following:

1. The delinquent land list would continue to be published twice in two newspapers, but errors in the first publication could be corrected in the second. The first publication would not have to be repeated.
2. The statute would clearly define tax foreclosure as an *in rem* procedure. Foreclosure proceedings would be brought against parcels of delinquent land only. The necessity of identifying all persons with an interest in the property and joining them as defendants is thus eliminated. Notice of foreclosure would be served through newspaper publication and a notice would be mailed to the last known owner of

the property as indicated by the general tax duplicate. This would remove the need for costly title search and notification efforts.

3. The prosecutor would be allowed to consolidate foreclosure actions for a large number of parcels into one action, which would reduce court costs substantially.

4. Tax delinquent property would be offered at foreclosure sales for at least the amount of delinquent taxes, assessments, penalties, costs, and current taxes due on the property. Delinquent property would no longer be appraised prior to sale, unless the court ordered an appraisal after the property had been unsuccessfully offered twice.

5. In municipalities that had elected to establish a Land Reutilization Program, title to delinquent property could be transferred to the municipality in lieu of foreclosure. The owner would be required to pay any foreclosure costs that had been incurred, and to prove that no other liens were held against the property.

6. In municipalities that had elected to establish a Land Reutilization Authority, delinquent vacant land and delinquent properties that contained condemned structures and, when offered at tax sales, failed to generate bids sufficient to cover taxes, assessments, penalties and costs, would be sold to the municipality. This would substantially reduce the volume of property to be offered at subsequent sales. Thus additional administrative and advertising costs would be avoided.

Issue 2: How Can the City and Other Taxing Districts Be Compensated for Lost Tax Revenues and Property Maintenance Expenditures?

The tax sale procedure aims at the recovery of delinquent tax revenue and the eventual return of land to tax-paying status. Frequently the prices for which land is sold at the tax sales fail to cover both the outstanding taxes, assessments, and penalties and the administrative costs incurred in bringing the parcels to sale. If a parcel is sold for less than the outstanding tax liens against it, the remainder of the taxes are abated. Any excess received over the amount of the outstanding public liens is returned to the property-owner or other lien holders.

Foreclosure sales of Cleveland properties have been yielding approximately one-third of the outstanding delinquent taxes. Net losses on the parcels that were sold at sheriff's sales from 1969 to 1971 were over $144,000, while $74,000 in delinquent taxes were recovered. Very few of the parcels offered at sheriff's sales actually sold, however. Substantial administrative costs were incurred on the parcels that did not sell—over

75 percent of those offered in 1973 and 1974. At the 1969 and 1972 forfeiture sales, slightly over $72,000 in delinquent taxes was recovered, but over $300,000 was abated on the 437 parcels that were sold. Actual administrative costs incurred to bring these parcels to the point of the forfeiture sale are not known; but at an estimated $400 per parcel, administrative costs would have totaled over $160,000.

Although the tax sale procedure was not recovering a substantial portion of outstanding taxes, its primary goal was to return nonproductive land to tax-paying status. The inability to recover all outstanding taxes and assessments at the sales could perhaps have been justified if the parcels had begun to produce tax revenue again. This was not the case in Cleveland. Parcels became delinquent again shortly after they were purchased at tax sales. Almost one-half of the parcels sold at tax foreclosure sales from 1969 to 1971 were delinquent again by 1973. Over 40 percent of the parcels sold at the 1973 and 1974 foreclosure sales, and almost 60 percent of the parcels sold at the forfeiture sales in 1969 and 1972, were delinquent again by December 1974.

The traditional tax foreclosure procedure failed to recover delinquent taxes and return land to the tax duplicate because it did not reflect the basic land market changes that have occurred in inner-city areas. Today property tax delinquency is often a result of more than an individual owner's personal financial difficulties. The bulk of the delinquent property in Cleveland is located in heavily deteriorated neighborhoods and currently has little potential for short-term reuse. Interest in the purchase of delinquent parcels at tax sales is limited because of the land's low value. It may be many years before there is again demand for land in these areas.

The structural abandonment occurring in several of Cleveland's neighborhoods is indicative of the low or negative market values of inner-city properties. Owners are finding that the operation of their properties is financially unprofitable because of the low available rents, high vacancies, and rising operating costs. Many are simply abandoning their properties because they no longer have value. Tax delinquency is but one of the manifestations of an abandonment decision that affects local government. Vandals often severely damage property soon after the last occupant departs. Arson is common in the structures, placing a burden on the fire department. Also, because owners rarely repair or demolish vandalized structures after they are condemned, the city is forced to raze them to protect the health and safety of those who remain in the neighborhood. Between 1966 and early 1974, the city of Cleveland spent over $4 million to demolish unsafe and vandalized buildings. Almost 60 percent of the structures on the city's 1973 and 1974 demolition lists were tax delinquent at the time of demolition. Many of the remainder became delinquent after they were razed because the owners failed to pay the demolition liens placed on the tax duplicate.

The public's investment in delinquent property is substantial. Under the historic procedure, foreclosed properties were sold, often at a loss, to individuals who frequently did not pay the property taxes on their new purchases. Eventually these properties underwent foreclosure again, requiring additional public expenditures for administrative costs.

Recommendations on Issue 2

To avoid the recycling of delinquent land through the foreclosure process and to provide some form of compensation for public investment in delinquent and abandoned property, we recommended that municipalities should have the option of establishing a Land Reutilization Program. Such a program would also facilitate the assembly of inner-city land for future redevelopment. Under this program, nonproductive lands for which adequate bids were not received at tax sales would be held in trust for the affected taxing districts by the municipality.

The Land Reutilization Program, which is similar to the program operating in St. Louis, Missouri, was envisioned as having the following characteristics:

1. A municipality would establish a Land Reutilization Program by enacting an ordinance that acknowledged the existence of a sufficient amount of nonproductive land within its boundaries to necessitate the implementation of a Land Reutilization Program.
2. Nonproductive land would include any parcel of land upon which foreclosure proceedings had been initiated and that was vacant or contained unoccupied condemned buildings.
3. The municipality would have the responsibility of identifying nonproductive parcels on foreclosure lists. Those parcels would be listed separately in advertisements for foreclosure sales, along with a notification that the city would bid the full amounts of liens and costs.
4. Nonproductive land could be sold to the municipality at the first tax sale if no other bids were received for at least the amount of delinquent taxes, assessments, penalties, and costs.
5. The administrative functions of the Land Reutilization Program would include:
   a. Management and maintenance of acquired property.
   b. Planning for potential present and future uses of the land.
   c. Disposition of property to fulfill the program's objectives.
   d. Maintenance of accounts of all expenditures and revenues associated with each individual parcel.

6. The Land Reutilization Program would have to sell property at its fair market value unless it was to be sold to a public body. The consent of all affected taxing subdivisions would be required prior to a transfer to a public body at less than fair market value.

7. A municipality that established a Land Reutilization Program would be required to set up an advisory committee composed of a representative of each taxing district with an interest in the property. This committee would be kept informed of the program's activities and advise the municipality on matters pertaining to the program's operation.

8. Property acquired by a Land Reutilization Program would be tax exempt until it was sold or leased.

9. The amount of the municipality's bid would not be payable until the sale of the property. The amount due would not exceed the proceeds of the sale. Sale proceeds would be distributed to the municipality to cover costs incurred for: administration of the program, maintenance of the property, costs of foreclosure, and outstanding taxes, assessments, and penalties.

Issue 3: Should a Municipal Land Reutilization Program Acquire Occupied Residential Properties?

Approximately 52 percent (5800) of the tax delinquent parcels in the city of Cleveland contained occupied buildings in 1975. About 2100 of these properties were located in relatively stable neighborhoods and would have had substantial market values. However, the other 3700, mostly residential buildings, were in neighborhoods in varying stages of decline. In 1975 these buildings contained over 10,000 housing units, of which an estimated 7300 were in deteriorated neighborhoods. Between 20 and 25 percent of the residential units located in declining areas were owner-occupied in 1975. Most of the remaining units were rented to low- and moderate-income tenants.

The economics of Cleveland's lower income housing market are such that rents do not cover the costs of operating buildings in standard condition. The disparity between revenues and costs is particularly great in buildings that are mortgaged. Landlords with lower income tenants have cut their costs by eliminating many maintenance expenditures and in some cases by failing to pay property taxes.

If a municipality were to acquire title to occupied residential property, experience with the Cuyahoga County tax sales indicates that it would be difficult if not impossible to find people interested in purchasing such buildings. Because standard housing for low-income tenants usually cannot be provided without substantial subsidies, the city would therefore be faced with the choice of operating substandard housing or subsidizing a significant portion of its residential inventory.

Recommendations on Issue 3

We concluded that it would be financially infeasible for a municipal Land Reutilization Program to acquire title to occupied residential structures. Municipalities cannot afford the level of subsidy required to maintain these units in standard condition, and adequate federal housing subsidies are not available.

Under the legislation that was proposed, the foreclosure process for improved residential properties that had not been condemned would be similar to the present procedure, with the modifications listed in the discussion of Issue 1. The streamlining of the process would accelerate foreclosure on the properties to some extent, as many administrative bottlenecks would be eliminated. However, occupied residential properties would continue to be offered at least twice at foreclosure sales. Any properties that remained unsold would then be offered at a forfeiture sale. The availability of extended contractual terms for repayment of delinquent taxes, as discussed in Issue 4, should help to minimize any hardships imposed on the occupants of delinquent properties.

Issue 4: How Can Any Hardships Imposed on Residential Property-Owners as a Result of Foreclosure Be Minimized?

Ohio's foreclosure laws allow a period of redemption prior to foreclosure, wherein an owner may pay outstanding taxes. Property cannot be foreclosed upon until it has been delinquent for at least two years. Delinquent taxes can be repaid in five consecutive, semiannual installments. A substantial number of owners of delinquent properties pay up their back taxes during the period of redemption. These owners have usually experienced temporary financial difficulties and are not part of the city's long-term tax delinquency problem. Approximately one-third of the parcels are redeemed within the first year after they are certified delinquent. An owner may also redeem property after foreclosure has been initiated.

As discussed earlier, many of the delinquent residential properties are occupied by low-income households. Many homeowners and landlords may not be able to repay their taxes in a lump sum. Allowing them to spread their payments over a longer period would perhaps make redemption easier in cases of particular financial difficulty.

Additional restrictions were required, however, to assure that the privilege to enter into a contract was not abused. An owner who wished to further postpone payment of taxes could enter into a contract, thus removing the property from the foreclosure process. Because of delays experienced in the processing of delinquent properties, foreclosure often was not initiated again immediately after default. Thus the owner could retain control of his or her property for additional time without repaying delinquent taxes.

Recommendations on Issue 4

Several provisions that addressed the above issues were proposed, including:

1. The provisions of the foreclosure statute that regulated redemption would be consolidated for the purpose of clarity.
2. Owners of delinquent property would continue to be allowed to enter into contracts for the payment of taxes in five semiannual payments. In cases of individual hardship, however, the court would be authorized to extend the installment contract on residential properties for an additional five semiannual payments.
3. If the owner of delinquent property wished to redeem the property or enter into a contract to pay the taxes after the commencement of foreclosure proceedings, a foreclosure judgment would have to be rendered. In addition, the property-owner would be required to pay the foreclosure costs.

We believe that the revisions of the Ohio foreclosure process serve to (1) markedly reduce administrative costs while still protecting property-owners' rights; (2) provide a form of compensation for the public's investment in delinquent properties; and (3) assist in the reutilization of presently nonproductive land.

The recommendations incorporated in the legislation recognize the constraints imposed on the process by the weakening of the land market and yet provide cost savings and operating efficiencies to those responsible for the administration of the foreclosure process. In addition, the Land Reutilization Program will assist the city of Cleveland in its future neighborhood redevelopment efforts. Because neither the tax delinquency problem nor our solutions are unique to Cleveland, the recommendations discussed here and presented in the final bill will also interest other jurisdictions confronted with increased tax delinquency on urban properties.

Appendixes

Table A-1
Population and Housing Characteristics, by Neighborhood Type, for Cleveland's Residential Statistical Areas

Statistical Area[a] Name and Number	Population Characteristics			Housing Characteristics				
	Population % Change, 1960–1970	Nonwhite as % of Total Population, 1970	Median Household Income, 1969	% of Single-Family Units	% of Owner-Occupied Units	Median Value of Owner-Occupied Structures	% of Occupied Units Overcrowded	New Units, 1960–1970, as % of All 1970 Units
Stage 1[b]								
West								
Riverside (39)	+17%	1%	$9,929	84.8%	75.9%	$21,400	8.2%	20.7%
Puritas-Bellaire-Longmead (38)	+ 1	8	10,157	87.1	84.9	18,200	8.7	12.9
Munn-Warren (37)	− 7	1	10,781	81.4	79.6	23,800	4.3	5.3
Jefferson (36)	− 1	0	9,518	71.2	68.7	18,300	4.3	7.6
Broadview-Schaaf (35)	+ 7	0	9,085	65.1	66.8	19,300	3.6	14.4
Memphis-Fulton (34)	− 5	0	9,396	72.0	70.7	19,400	3.1	4.4
Clark-Fulton (33)	−11	0	8,125	42.8	54.1	13,400	6.3	2.2
Denison (32)	−12	2	7,641	44.0	45.9	14,900	6.1	7.4
Midwest South (29)	− 1	0	9,269	58.1	59.5	16,900	4.7	4.7
Edgewater (28)***	+ 3	2	7,560	28.9	27.6	18,600	3.2	14.8
East								
North Collinwood-Wildwood (1)	− 5	3	8,757	53.3	55.9	18,500	2.8	12.8
Euclid (3)	+13	2	8,830	51.4	42.9	18,900	2.8	21.9
Harvard-Lee (18)	+ 5	92	11,970	98.4	96.3	20,200	7.1	9.9
Stage 1.5								
West								
Midwest North (27)***	−16	1	8,189	44.7	43.8	14,800	6.1	3.7
East								
South Broadway (22)	−15	1	7,906	39.4	49.1	13,000	6.2	0.7
Corlett (20)	+ 8	79	8,565	64.7	73.2	16,500	8.7	3.7
Lee-Seville-Miles (19)	+19	98	9,844	88.0	81.1	18,000	11.9	28.1
Mt. Pleasant (17)	− 8	96	7,078	35.3	49.3	16,000	7.0	2.6
Shaker Square (15)	− 3	28	7,931	24.1	34.0	18,800	2.7	6.1
Norwood (6)***	−12	25	6,252	30.8	35.8	11,000	7.8	0.2

142

Stage 2							
West							
Near West Side (26)	− 7	6	5,387	26.2	22.9	10,800	10.7	10.3
East							
Miles-Warner (21)	−15	15	8,521	59.1	67.6	15,900	7.0	1.2
Paul Revere (16)	+ 6	68	7,974	53.7	66.1	15,200	8.7	2.5
Woodland Hills (14)	−18	40	6,528	25.8	40.4	14,000	5.7	1.7
University Circle (10)	−21	28	2,502	18.9	23.0	12,300	3.9	0.1
Goodrich (7)	−33	5	5,752	28.2	25.7	9,500	6.9	0.6
South Collinwood (2)	− 9	24	7,844	44.1	45.4	14,900	6.1	2.5
Stage 2.5							
West							
Fulton-Train (30)***	−29	1	7,214	36.2	36.3	13,700	11.5	0.7
East							
North Broadway (23)***	−23	2	7,554	45.2	51.0	10,700	8.2	1.4
Forest Hills (4)	+ 8	98	7,629	46.1	41.2	14,300	10.3	0.4
Stage 3							
West							
Tremont (31)	−33	4	6,155	28.2	30.6	9,500	10.8	1.6
East							
Kinsman (13)	−25	91	3,928	27.3	22.4	9,400	14.0	11.7
East Central (11)	−29	94	3,926	24.8	22.5	11,200	8.0	0.4
Glenville (5)	−15	96	6,245	41.3	41.1	14,000	9.4	0.6
Stage 4							
East							
East Hough (9)	−30	93	3,862	22.2	19.1	12,300	10.8	7.4
West Hough (8)	−43	94	3,377	19.7	16.6	10,000	14.6	0.5
Stage 4.5							
East							
West Central (12)	−49	90	3,196	22.3	8.0	8,900	12.8	7.5

Source: U.S. Census, 1970; Cleveland City Planning Commission.

[a]For the location of specific statistical areas, see Figure 4-2.

[b]For a description of the stages of neighborhood development used to categorize Cleveland's residential statistical areas, see Table 4-1.

***Within this area, there is more qualitative variation from census tract to census tract than in most of the other areas, which are highly homogeneous.

Table A-2
Total Number of Tax Delinquent Parcels, by Residential Statistical Area

Statistical Area Name and Number[a]	1966 Number	1966 % of All Parcels	1970 Number	1970 % of All Parcels	1974 Number	1974 % of All Parcels	% Change, 1966–1974
Stage I[b]							
West							
Riverside (39)	150	2.3%	142	2.2%	115	1.7%	-23.3%
Puritas-Bellaire-Longmead (38)	375	3.9	288	3.0	294	3.0	-21.6
Munn-Warren (37)	53	1.5	51	1.4	40	1.1	-24.5
Jefferson (36)	101	1.4	91	1.3	107	1.5	5.9
Broadview-Schaaf (35)	168	2.3	200	2.7	145	2.0	-13.7
Memphis-Fulton (34)	64	1.2	60	1.1	58	1.1	-9.4
Clark-Fulton (33)	112	2.0	135	2.4	157	2.8	40.2
Denison (32)	134	2.9	113	2.4	133	2.8	-0.7
Midwest South (29)	77	1.6	68	1.4	64	1.3	-16.9
Edgewater (28)	48	2.5	54	2.8	53	2.8	10.4
East							
North Collinwood-Wildwood (1)	181	2.6	163	2.3	201	2.9	11.0
Euclid (3)	52	2.5	44	2.1	51	2.5	- 1.9
Harvard-Lee (18)	188	3.9	184	3.8	170	3.5	- 9.6
Stage 1.5							
West							
Midwest North (27)	155	2.5	178	3.0	198	3.3	27.7
East							
South Broadway (22)	201	3.1	200	3.1	226	3.5	12.4
Corlett (20)	152	2.9	142	2.7	199	3.8	30.9
Lee-Seville-Miles (19)	401	15.0	327	12.8	334	13.0	-16.7
Mt. Pleasant (17)	345	4.7	336	4.6	437	5.9	26.7
Shaker Square (15)	76	2.5	71	2.4	111	3.7	46.1
Norwood (6)	118	2.8	156	3.7	352	8.3	198.3

Stage 2							
West							
Near West Side (26)	175	4.7	175	4.7	225	6.1	28.6
East							
Miles-Warner (21)	121	3.5	142	4.1	199	5.8	64.5
Paul Revere (16)	89	2.7	136	4.1	188	5.7	111.2
Woodland Hills (14)	83	2.6	92	2.9	168	5.4	102.4
University Circle (10)	118	6.3	133	7.2	132	7.2	11.9
Goodrich (7)	100	4.2	100	4.2	97	4.1	– 3.0
South Collinwood (2)	168	3.3	190	3.8	260	5.2	54.8
Stage 2.5							
West							
Fulton-Train (30)	160	3.9	173	4.2	224	5.5	40.0
East							
North Broadway (23)	181	4.7	148	3.9	167	4.4	– 7.7
Forest Hills (4)	150	2.8	212	4.0	355	6.7	136.7
Stage 3							
West							
Tremont (31)	253	6.2	247	6.1	320	7.8	26.5
East							
Kinsman (13)	203	12.5	252	15.8	361	22.7	77.8
East Central (11)	727	14.5	878	17.7	1,090	21.9	49.9
Glenville (5)	604	7.8	748	9.9	1,103	14.5	82.6
Stage 4							
East							
East Hough (9)	347	8.7	549	14.9	765	21.0	120.2
West Hough (8)	472	14.4	721	22.6	1,015	32.0	115.0
Stage 4.5							
East							
West Central (12)	924	19.6	922	21.0	998	23.4	8.0

Source: Cleveland City Planning Commission, Real Estate Research Corporation.

[a]For the location of specific statistical areas, see Figure 4–2.

[b]For a description of the stages of neighborhood development used to categorize Cleveland's statistical areas, see Table 4–1.

Table A-3
Families Receiving Aid to Dependent Children (ADC) in Cleveland's Residential Statistical Areas

Statistical Area[a] Name and Number	% of All Families Receiving ADC, 1970	% of All Families Receiving ADC, November 1974
Stage 1[b]		
West		
Riverside (39)	2.6%	4.7%
Puritas-Bellaire-Longmead (38)	1.0	4.2
Munn-Warren (37)	0.2	0.9
Jefferson (36)	1.0	6.5
Broadview-Schaaf (35)	1.0	2.5
Memphis-Fulton (34)	3.8	2.4
Clark-Fulton (33)	3.8	10.3
Midwest South (29)	1.6	4.6
Edgewater (28)	2.1	5.8
Denison (32)	4.3	11.0
East		
North Collinwood-Wildwood (1)	1.3	4.1
Euclid (3)	1.0	3.9
Harvard-Lee (18)	2.3	7.2
Stage 1.5		
West		
Midwest North (27)	3.8	12.3
East		
South Broadway (22)	3.1	7.9
Lee-Seville-Miles (19)	6.4	18.7
Mount Pleasant (17)	12.4	23.4
Shaker Square (15)	2.4	9.9
Norwood (6)	11.2	20.5
Corlett (20)	7.7	22.6
Stage 2		
West		
Near West Side (26)	13.8	26.0
East		
Miles-Warner (21)	4.7	22.2
Paul Revere (16)	11.3	28.5

Table A–3 Continued

Statistical Area[a] Name and Number	% of All Families Receiving ADC, 1970	% of All Families Receiving ADC, November 1974
Woodland Hills (14)	12.2	37.1
University Circle (10)	9.7	16.0
Goodrich (7)	7.0	13.3
South Collinwood (2)	7.2	19.8
Stage 2.5		
West		
Fulton-Train (30)	10.9	20.7
East		
North Broadway (23)	5.8	11.2
Forest Hills (4)	22.4	32.5
Stage 3		
West		
Tremont (31)	14.5	23.8
East		
Kinsman (13)	28.3	37.5
East Central (11)	25.8	32.8
Glenville (5)	26.6	32.0
Stage 4		
East		
East Hough (9)	34.1	37.3
West Hough (8)	41.0	41.4
Stage 4.5		
East		
West Central (12)	33.9	47.5

Source: City of Cleveland Planning Commission.

[a]For the location of specific statistical areas, see Figure 4-2.

[b]For a description of the stages of neighborhood development used to categorize Cleveland's residential statistical areas, see Table 4–1.

Table A–4
Vacant Delinquent Land in Field Survey Neighborhoods

Statistical Area Name and Number	Total Delinquent Parcels	Vacant Delinquent Parcels	
		Number	% of Total Delinquent Parcels
Stage 1			
Denison (32)	133	39	29.3%
Puritas-Bellaire-Longmead (38)	294	156	53.1[a]
Stage 1.5			
Shaker Square (15)	112	12	10.7
Lee-Seville-Miles (19)	334	226	67.7[a]
Stage 2			
South Collinwood (2)	260	76	29.2
Woodland Hills (14)	168	36	21.4
Paul Revere (16)	188	69	36.7
Miles-Warner (21)	199	87	43.7
Stage 2.5			
Forest Hills (4)	355	106	29.8
Stage 3			
Glenville (5)	1103	308	27.9
East Central (11)	1090	416	38.2
Kinsman (13)	361	170	47.1
Tremont (31)	321	184	57.3
Stage 4			
West Hough (8)	1015	590	58.1
Total surveyed areas	5933	2475	41.7%

Source: 1974 Cuyahoga County Auditor's Billing Tapes.

[a]Puritas-Bellaire-Longmead and Lee-Seville-Miles are atypical neighborhoods with unusually high proportions of vacant delinquent parcels for neighborhoods in Stages 1 and 1.5, respectively. Puritas-Bellaire-Longmead has the only public and federally subsidized housing on the West Side, which somewhat distorts the characteristics of the predominantly stable neighborhood. Lee-Seville-Miles is a unique neighborhood with an almost rural character, a long-established, isolated, black community, and a large percentage of undeveloped land.

149

Table A–5
Relative and Absolute Physical Condition of Occupied Delinquent Residential Structures

All Types of Structures	Relative Condition			Absolute Condition			
	Better than Adjacent Buildings	Same as Adjacent Buildings	Worse than Adjacent Buildings	1—Good Condition	2—Fairly Good Condition	3—Deterioration Apparent	4—Dilapidated
Stage 1	3.8%	88.7%	7.5%	31.6%	55.7%	12.7%	0.0%
Stage 1.5	1.4	89.3	9.3	31.4	59.3	8.6	0.7
Stage 2	3.8	90.4	5.8	15.5	66.4	17.8	0.3
Stage 2.5	6.9	79.3	13.8	13.3	62.8	22.9	1.0
Stage 3	11.1	71.7	17.2	17.2	55.3	25.7	1.8
Stage 4	16.0	61.3	22.7	8.2	67.4	23.7	0.7
Total survey	9.2%	76.1%	14.7%	16.7%	60.3%	21.9%	1.1%

Source: Cleveland City Planning Commission field survey.

Table A–6
Relative and Absolute Physical Condition of Vacant Delinquent Residential Structures

All Types of Structures	Relative Condition			Absolute Condition				
	Better than Adjacent Buildings	Same as Adjacent Buildings	Worse than Adjacent Buildings	1—Good Condition	2—Fairly Good Condition	3—Deterioration Apparent	4—Dilapidated	5—Open and Vandalized
Stage 1	0.0%	33.3%	66.7%	0.0%	33.3%	66.7%	0.0%	0.0%
Stage 1.5	0.0	33.3	66.7	0.0	33.3	46.7	20.0	0.0
Stage 2	0.0	59.4	40.6	3.1	34.4	28.1	21.9	12.5
Stage 2.5	0.0	31.6	68.4	0.0	21.1	36.8	15.8	26.3
Stage 3	0.9	30.3	68.8	1.8	16.1	29.5	10.7	41.9
Stage 4	3.3	8.2	88.5	3.3	11.9	11.9	11.9	61.0
Total survey	1.2%	28.9%	69.9%	2.1%	19.2%	27.1%	13.3%	38.3%

Source: Cleveland City Planning Commission field survey.

Table A-7
Surveyed Tax Delinquent Parcels with Occupied Structures, by Use of Structure

Use of Structure	% of Total Sample Properties with Occupied Structures
Residential	88.2%
Mixed residential and commercial	2.6
Commercial	8.0
Industrial	0.4
Public utility	0.0
Institutional	0.8
Total occupied sample properties	100.0%

Source: Cleveland City Planning Commission field survey, Summer 1975.

Appendix B

Summary of Ohio H. B. 1327 As Enacted Into Law

Purpose

The stated purposes of the bill are to establish a workable method of restoring tax delinquent property to the tax rolls and to help rejuvenate and redevelop abandoned areas of cities.

Content and Operation

The bill states that all of its provisions apply to proceedings pending or in progress on the effective date of the bill, but that all actions already taken in the proceedings are to remain in full effect and force.

Foreclosure and Forfeiture

(Existing law requires that proceedings for foreclosure of tax liens be instituted and prosecuted in the same manner provided by law for the foreclosure of mortgages on land. This means that the county prosecuting attorney is required to identify, by title search or otherwise, all persons who appear to have any right, title, and interest in or lien upon the property being foreclosed, to join all of them as defendants, and to obtain service of process on all such defendants in the manner required by applicable rules of civil procedure.)

The delinquent land list and duplicate prepared by the auditor shall contain the name of the person as it is listed on the tax list as of the date of certification of the delinquent list.

The auditor may correct any errors appearing in the first publication of the delinquent tax list in the second publication of the list without peril to the required number of publications.

The bill establishes a specific statutory procedure for tax foreclosure proceedings on parcels that have been certified delinquent for at least three years, by making these foreclosure actions *in rem* actions. *In rem,* in this context, means that all persons in the world are bound to know that the property may be sold, without notice, other than by newspaper publication, to anyone except the person shown as the owner on the tax records. The change eliminates the current requirements of identifying and joining individual defendants.

151

To begin an *in rem* foreclosure proceeding under the bill, the county prosecutor must file a complaint with the clerk of a court of competent jurisdiction. Each parcel included in a complaint must be given a serial number and be separately indexed and docketed by the clerk in a special book.

The complaint must contain:

1. The permanent parcel number for each parcel
2. The full street address, when available
3. The description of each parcel in the delinquent land tax certificate
4. The name and address of the last known owner if they appear on the general tax list
5. The amount of taxes, assessments, and penalties due on the parcel
6. The allegation that a delinquent land tax certificate has been filed by the county auditor for each parcel
7. The allegation that the amount due is unpaid and a lien against the property
8. The prayer of the complaint that the court make an order that the parcels be sold by foreclosure sale

The bill contains the form that is to be substantially followed in filing the complaint.

Within thirty days after a complaint has been filed, the clerk of courts must have a notice of foreclosure published once a week for three consecutive weeks in a newspaper of general circulation in the county. (The bill provides the form that the notice must follow.) After the last publication, the newspaper publisher must file an affidavit with the clerk showing that the notice was published and including a copy of the published notice.

The clerk must also send, within thirty days of the filing of the complaint, a notice to each person listed in the complaint as the last known owner. If the name and address are not given in the complaint because they did not appear on the last general tax list, the auditor must file an affidavit with the clerk.

Any person owning or claiming any right, title, or interest in, or lien upon any parcel can file an answer with the clerk of court within sixty days or the first publication of notice of foreclosure. The answer must contain (1) the caption and number of the case; (2) the serial number of the parcel; (3) the nature and amount of interest claimed; and (4) any defense or objection to the foreclosing of the state's lien for delinquent taxes, assessments, penalties, and charges contained in the complaint.

A copy of the answer must also be served on the county prosecutor within sixty days of the first publication of the notice.

A default judgment may be taken on any parcel listed in the complaint for which no answer is filed within sixty days. Such a judgment is valid and effective even though the owner or person claiming right, title, interest, or lien is a minor, incompetent, absentee, or nonresident of the state, or a convict in confinement.

At the foreclosure trial, the delinquent land tax certificate that was filed by the auditor with the prosecutor is considered under the bill to be prima-facie evidence of the amount and validity of the taxes, assessments, penalties, and charges due on the parcel. If an answer is properly filed, the court must, if requested by the answering defendant, separate the parcel from the foreclosure proceedings. The court also is authorized to separate the parcel even if the answering defendant does not request it.

The bill requires that the court make a finding on each parcel for the amount of taxes, assessments, penalties, costs, and charges due. The total amount is the minimum figure for which the property is to be sold. Unless the court orders some parcels to be sold together, each parcel must be sold separately.

The officer to whom the sale is directed must advertise the sale once a week for three consecutive weeks. Any number of parcels can be included in the advertisement. The notice must contain the date, time, and place of a second sale, to be held at least two but not more than six weeks after the first sale if the parcel is not sold at the first sale. (The bill provides the form of the notice.)

If there are no bids at the first sale equal to the amount of taxes, assessments, penalties, and costs due on a parcel, the officer must adjourn the sale of the parcel to the date of the second sale. If the parcel is not sold at the second sale, the officer conducting the sale must report that to the court.

The court may, in its discretion, order any parcel not sold to be readvertised and appraised, with the court setting a minimum price for the parcel.

Under existing law, upon confirmation of a sale, the proceeds must be applied in the following order of payment (1) all costs; (2) amount found due for taxes, assessments, and charges; and (3) amount of taxes and assessments accruing after the entry of finding and before the sale.

Under the existing law, the conveyance of a parcel while it is under foreclosure proceedings requires that a new foreclosure action be brought against the new owner. The bill provides that the foreclosing proceedings are not nullified by conveyance by the owner of the parcel during the time from the first publication of the delinquent tax list up to the foreclosure judgment.

Existing law permits redemption of delinquent land before foreclosure proceedings are begun by payment to the county treasurer of the amount due. The bill extends the time allowed for redemption by permitting redemption during the period between the beginning of foreclosure proceedings and confirmation of the foreclosure sale, upon payment to the treasurer of all amounts due. The bill also permits the amount due to be paid after the foreclosure judgment and before the foreclosure sale in five consecutive and substantially equal semiannual installments upon written agreement with the county treasurer. The current taxes and assessments must be paid as they come due.

Upon application to the court, and if it can be shown that it would prevent hardship, the court can extend the installment terms on delinquent land devoted to residential use to up to ten payments. If any payment is not made, the treasurer is required to advise the court of the fact and the court is then required to order the land sold for the amount of taxes, assessments, penalties, and charges then due. Until the total amount is paid, the court retains jurisdiction over the land, even if it is conveyed to another owner.

Whenever an installment payment is made, the county treasurer must enter and credit the amount on the tax duplicate and give the person a receipt on a form prescribed by the state auditor.

Under the existing law, any tax delinquent land offered for sale under the Foreclosure Law on two occasions at least four weeks apart that does not receive any minimum bids is forfeited to the state. The forfeited land remains on the tax lists and the county auditor must offer the land for sale annually. The bill does not change the existing forfeiture procedures.

Land Reutilization Program (LRP)

This portion of the bill establishes a mechanism through which any municipal corporation can undertake a program to aid in the return of "nonproductive" tax delinquent land to the tax rolls.

"Nonproductive" land is defined by the bill as any parcel of delinquent land on which foreclosure proceedings have begun and on which there are either (1) no buildings or other structures; or (2) unoccupied buildings or other structures against which the municipal corporation has instituted proceedings (under section 715.26 of the Revised Code or Section 3 of Article XVIII of the Ohio Constitution) for removal or demolition of the building or other structure because of its unsafe, insecure, or defective condition.

"Occupancy" is defined as the actual, continuous, and exclusive use and possession of a parcel by a person having a lawful right to such use and possession.

A municipal corporation can begin a "Land Reutilization Program" (hereafter referred to as LRP) by enacting an ordinance stating that the existence of nonproductive land in the municipal corporation necessitates implementation of an LRP to foster the return of the land to tax revenue generating status or for public use. The municipal corporation must then promptly deliver certified copies of the ordinance to the county auditor, treasurer, and prosecutor. From the effective date of the ordinance, all foreclosure, sale, management, and disposition of nonproductive land in the municipal corporation must be governed by the provisions of the bill relating to LRPs.

Upon receipt of the ordinance, the county prosecutor must compile and deliver a list of all delinquent lands in the municipal corporation against which foreclosure proceedings have been instituted or are pending. The municipal corporation must then determine whether any of the lands are "nonproductive" and notify the prosecutor prior to advertisement and sale of the lands. All nonproductive lands identified by the municipal corporation must be advertised separately from other delinquent lands, and the advertisement must contain the notice that if the nonproductive lands do not receive a minimum bid at sale, they will be sold to the municipal corporation.

If the nonproductive lands do not receive a minimum bid at the foreclosure sale after the second offering, the municipal corporation is considered to have submitted a minimum bid. The officer conducting the sale must announce the municipal corporation's bid at the sale and report it to the court for confirmation of sale. The amount bid by the municipal corporation, however, is not payable until the land is sold or otherwise disposed of by the municipal corporation under its LRP and then can be paid only from the proceeds of the sale.

Upon confirmation of sale of any nonproductive lands to a municipal corporation, the court costs initially must be paid by the municipal corporation to the county treasury. The amount must then be apportioned among the taxing districts having an interest in the delinquent taxes, assessments, and penalties, and returned to the municipal corporation by the county from the next tax settlement for each taxing district.

Upon confirmation, the title to the land passes to the municipal corporation free of all liens and encumbrances except easements and covenants of record. The title cannot be ruled invalid because of any irregularity, informality, or omission of any foreclosure proceedings or process of taxation if the irregularity, informality, or omission did not abrogate the notice provisions to persons having right, title, or interest in the land.

Upon receipt of the ordinance establishing an LRP, the county auditor must give the municipal corporation a list of all delinquent lands in the municipal corporation that have forfeited to the state. (Under existing law, any tax delinquent land offered for sale under the Foreclosure Law on two occasions at least four weeks apart that receives no bids is forfeited to the state. The forfeited lands remain on the tax lists and the county auditor must offer the lands for sale annually.) From the auditor's list of forfeited lands, the municipal corporation must determine the nonproductive lands, and notify the auditor. In any future sales of the forfeited lands, the auditor must advertise the nonproductive lands separately from other forfeited lands and include in the advertisement a notice that if there is no minimum bid, the lands will be sold to the municipal corporation.

If no bid sufficient to pay taxes, assessments, penalties, and costs (under existing procedures the minimum bid was $10) is received at the forfeiture sale, the land is sold to the municipal corporation for the minimum amount, but the amount is not payable until the land is sold or otherwise disposed of by the municipal corporation under its LRP and then can only be paid from the proceeds of the sale.

The auditor must then give the municipal corporation a deed giving the municipal corporation clear title to the land except for taxes and special assessments not due at the time of sale, and easements and covenants made before the foreclosure proceedings. Costs must be initially paid by the municipal corporation and then apportioned by the auditor among all taxing subdivisions having an interest in the unpaid taxes, assessments, and penalties. The county then retains the amount from the next tax disbursal and credits it to the municipal corporation's general fund.

The bill provides that any action or defense questioning the validity of the municipal corporation's title to the land for any irregularity, informality, or omission in the foreclosure or forfeiture proceedings must be started within one year of the filing of the deed.

The bill requires that the municipal corporation hold and administer any property it acquires for its LRP for the benefit of itself and any other taxing subdivision that has an interest in it. The municipal corporation is required to do the following:

1. Manage, maintain, and protect the lands in such manner as it considers appropriate.
2. Compile and maintain a written inventory of the lands, which is to be available to the public.
3. Study, analyze, and evaluate potential uses of the lands.
4. Plan for and encourage the sale or other disposition of the lands as appropriate to the purpose of the LRP.
5. Establish and maintain records and accounts of all transactions, ex-

penditures, and revenues relating to the LRP, including separate itemizations for each parcel of land.

The bill permits the municipal corporation to sell any land in its LRP to private interests at any time without competitive bidding, provided that the price is not less than fair market value. The municipal corporation can, with approval of the legislative authorities of all taxing subdivisions entitled to share in the proceeds of the sale, devote the lands to public use and use the land itself or sell, lease, or transfer the land at less than fair market value to another political subdivision.

If the municipal corporation desires, it can consolidate or subdivide parcels in order to assemble workable tracts of land.

When a municipal corporation sells or disposes of land under its LRP, the proceeds must be distributed in the following order of payment:

1. To the municipal corporation for reimbursement of costs incurred in the acquisition, maintenance, and disposal of the land, and the parcel's share of the LRP costs.
2. To the county treasurer for proportional distribution to taxing subdivisions to which the county auditor apportioned costs of foreclosure or forfeiture.
3. To the county treasurer for distribution to taxing subdivisions entitled to participate in the taxes, assessments, and penalties due on the land up to the time it was acquired by the municipal corporation, and the amount of taxes, assessments, and penalties that would have accrued if the land had not been tax exempt after it was acquired by the municipal corporation

Any balance remaining after these distributions have been made is to be retained by the municipal corporation for its LRP.

The bill requires the municipal corporation to keep interested taxing subdivisions informed about the administration of its LRP and to establish a committee made up of one representative per taxing subdivision having an interest in the taxes, assessments, and penalties due on land in the LRP. The committee members, who can be employees of their respective subdivisions, must be appointed by their subdivisions and serve without compensation. The committee must meet at least quarterly to advise the municipal corporation on any matter related to its LRP.

In addition, the municipal corporation is required to establish neighborhood advisory committees, appointed by the Mayor, for consultation and advice regarding the program. The committees would consist of five to nine residents or property owners in areas affected by the program.

With the consent of the county auditor, a municipal corporation can accept a conveyance in lieu of foreclosure of any tax delinquent land to the municipal corporation's LRP from the owners upon payment by the owners or the municipal corporation of all expenses incurred by the county in connection with foreclosure proceedings. However, the municipal corporation must receive satisfactory evidence that it will obtain fee simple title free of all liens and encumbrances except the lien for delinquent taxes, assessment, penalties, and charges and for taxes and assessments not yet due. On the date of acquisition of the land by the municipal corporation, the lien for delinquent taxes, assessments, and penalties is removed.

All lands acquired and held by a municipal corporation in its LRP are declared by the bill to be public property used for a public purpose and therefore exempt from taxes until sold, leased, or transferred by the municipal corporation.

Under the bill, all land that remains in the LRP for fifteen years must be sold by the municipal corporation at public auction during the sixteenth year. If it is not sold then, it must be offered every three years thereafter until it is sold. The minimum acceptable bid must be the higher of the following two amounts: (1) two-thirds of the fair market value; or (2) the total amount of accrued taxes, assessments, penalties, costs, charges incurred by the municipal corporation in acquiring, maintaining and disposing of the parcel, and the parcel's share of the costs of the LRP.

A municipal corporation can discontinue its LRP by repealing the ordinance that created it, but the program must continue until all lands acquired under it are disposed of.

Other Provisions of the Bill

The bill adds a provision that requires a notice to be printed on all real estate tax bills stating that, if the taxes are not paid within one year from their due date, the property is subject to foreclosure for tax delinquency under Chapter 5721 of the Revised Code. It also states that failure to provide this notice will have no effect on the validity of tax foreclosure proceedings.

The bill changes the requirements that mortgage foreclosure must be published once a week for five weeks. It reduces the notice requirement to three weeks to conform with the tax foreclosure provisions.

If nonproductive land is subsequently included in an official impacted cities project, taxes on the land in the base period of the year immediately preceding the initial acquisition are determined by applying the greater valuation in either (a) the year preceding initial acquisition; or (b) the next succeeding year after such nonproductive land is sold.

About the Authors

Susan J. Olson, is a planner on the staff of the Cleveland City Planning Commission. In addition to her work on property tax delinquency and neighborhood abandonment, she has been involved in analyses of the fiscal impact of the city's redevelopment efforts. Ms. Olson received the M.C.P. degree from Ohio State University.

M. Leanne Lachman, a Vice President of Real Estate Research Corporation, is an economic and policy planner specializing in urban affairs. She is an ongoing consultant to the U. S. Department of Housing and Urban Development and to several city governments. Ms. Lachman has written numerous articles and reviews and is co-author with Al Smith and Anthony Downs of *Achieving Effective Desegregation,* which is also published by Lexington Books.